ISBN 978-1-333-16915-2
PIBN 10505947

1 MONTH OF
FREE
READING

at

www.ForgottenBooks.com

By purchasing this book you are eligible for one month membership to ForgottenBooks.com, giving you unlimited access to our entire collection of over 700,000 titles via our web site and mobile apps.

To claim your free month visit:

www.forgottenbooks.com/free505947

English
Français
Deutsche
Italiano
Español
Português

www.forgottenbooks.com

Mythology Photography **Fiction**
Fishing Christianity **Art** Cooking
Essays Buddhism Freemasonry
Medicine **Biology** Music **Ancient
Egypt** Evolution Carpentry Physics
Dance Geology **Mathematics** Fitness
Shakespeare **Folklore** Yoga Marketing
Confidence Immortality Biographies
Poetry **Psychology** Witchcraft
Electronics Chemistry History **Law**
Accounting **Philosophy** Anthropology
Alchemy Drama Quantum Mechanics
Atheism Sexual Health **Ancient History**
Entrepreneurship Languages Sport
Paleontology Needlework Islam
Metaphysics Investment Archaeology
Parenting Statistics Criminology
Motivational

Date Due

MAY 1 0 1944		
MAY 6 1945 D		
APR 2 7 1954 H V		
APR 3 1956 J N		
JAN 4 1960 C W		
FEB 1 1960 B N		
MAY 1 0 1962 E N		
MAR 1 1 1964 H O		
APR 2 1 1965 M P		
MAY 1 0 1965 M R		

NELSON

His Life
as told by Himself

GALE & POLDEN, LTD.,
2 Amen Corner, London, E.C.4.
Aldershot and Portsmouth

Portrait of Lord Nelson.

NELSON:
HIS LIFE AS TOLD BY HIMSELF.

BY

CLARA E. E. GYE.

LONDON:
GALE & POLDEN, LTD.,
2, AMEN CORNER, PATERNOSTER ROW, E.C.,
NELSON WORKS, PORTSMOUTH;
AND WELLINGTON WORKS, ALDERSHOT.

M

ALDERSHOT :

PRINTED BY GALE & POLDEN, LTD., WELLINGTON WORKS.

—

1905.

P-518.

Dedicated

AUTHOR'S NOTE.

THE excuse for this small work, if repetition on so great a subject need excuse, is the author's belief that in too many of the earlier Biographies and in some later Histories of Nelson, contemporary gossip, prejudices, and opinions, have been permitted so to colour many of the actual facts, that his character has in consequence been misjudged by both writers and readers. Also that these volumes have been made too lengthy for much popular or scholastic utility, in which direction the author hopes this abridged story may be found useful.

The aim of the writer has been to make Nelson speak for himself, and to add nothing which cannot be substantiated by his own words and writings, or by testimony which will not be questioned.

Under such curtailment a considerable amount of interesting matter has, of necessity, been left out, and therefore readers who wish to inquire further are referred to the works of Professor Laughton, Mr. G. Lathom Browne, Mr. W. Clark Russell, and to the Naval History of Mr. William James. To each of these writers the author is gratefully indebted for most facts and quotations herein contained.

HORATIO : VISCOUNT NELSON.

IN a small Parsonage house, in the year 1758, first saw the light England's hero, Horatio Nelson. It might almost be said England's greatest hero, for in all history it is hard to find one more truly great than the man whose heart not only prompted the famous watchword at Trafalgar, but whose whole life had been spent in acting up to it. The author thinks that a few more words here which may be said on the intention of this little book, will assist the reader in understanding the points which it is hoped to bring out in the following pages.

In most of the works on Nelson great stress, and justly so, has been laid on his genius, his bravery in action, fore-thought in all his preparations, and steadfast adherence to his duty, as an officer, a gentleman, and an Englishman ; but beyond all this, it may be said, adequate weight has not been given to that resolute force in his character, that great moral courage, so clearly shown in the manner by which he was enabled to distinguish between the duty of strict obedience to orders, and, at critical moments, the even higher duty of *dis*-obedience to orders. To quote only those instances which are the best known, he refused at Copenhagen to " Leave off Action," as signalled by the Commander-in-Chief ; and he defied everybody in the West Indies in the interests of the State.

In the face of every possible impediment from the people of the West India Islands, and even that of his own Commander-in-Chief, he insisted on the Navigation Laws being carried out, and the relaxation of them which, from interested motives had been silently allowed to increase, he stopped with a strong hand.

The Home Government ultimately ratified his action, and

it is to be hoped that (though the author finds no evidence
of this) the Home Authorities realised, that alongside this
fearless patriotism, and dauntless self-reliance, Nelson
possessed a disinterested unselfishness which is as great as
it is rare.

The Americans alone would have paid him immense
sums of money if he would have allowed these laws to lapse
entirely.

In any event Nelson never counted the cost to himself.
He frankly and fearlessly took on his own shoulders not
only the responsibility of the disregard of orders, but also
that of the consequences of his own action, and he carried
out his convictions through every difficulty, and against all
opposition.

After the battle of St. Vincent, however, where he
commanded the "Captain" (as Admiral the Hon. Sir
E. R. Fremantle has lately written) "he immediately
grasped the situation, and brilliantly disobeyed orders," his
Commander-in-Chief, Lord St. Vincent, nobly upheld him,
as will be told later on.

That so independent and successful a spirit should be
misunderstood as well as envied, by its contemporaries, was
perhaps inevitable, and there is evidence that Nelson's
warm and honest heart often ached through the rebuffs he
encountered, caused by the jealousies and misconstructions
against which he had to struggle.   These were shamefully
rife from time to time in the Government, and even at the
Admiralty itself—surely the first place where his great
services ought promptly and fully to have been recognised
in the beginning, and as completely, as his illustrious
conduct forced the Admiralty authorities to do in the end.

Nelson's first thought, from the outset of his career to
his last dying moments, was that England not only
" expected," but " demanded," that he should " do his duty."

It was that constant, inflexible intention of his which
gave him such power over those around him, and those
under his command.

In his letters and despatches his "King and Country," "the service," "his ship," and his "duty" are invariably first and foremost; himself, his private interests and predilections, second. The latter are never for one moment taken into the smallest consideration where "England's" interests and his own "duty" are concerned.

He had from his birth more than usual disadvantages against which to struggle, principally in his own weak health, his father's reduced circumstances, and the consequent necessity entailed by the latter that at the earliest possible moment each son should go out into the world to win his own bread, if not to contribute towards the maintenance of those at home.

He was, therefore, forced very early in life to concentrate his energies and to lose no opportunity of rising and succeeding in his profession. And success he won, early enough, due entirely to his own exertions, for at the age of 21 he was a post captain, and despite much opposition and undeserved neglect from the Admiralty authorities, and some others in high command, he won his way, sustained by the conviction that his duty was always done to the best of his ability, and that the day would come when he would be recognised for what he knew himself to be.

While still young he once wrote in a moment of revolt against an injustice done to him, "never mind, I will have a *Gazette* of my own one day." And in how many glorious instances was his prediction verified!

As an officer and a seaman the Admiralty were forced to depend on him and to recognise him as the mainstay of the English navy, notwithstanding that there were, at that time many great and highly capable commanders.

As a diplomatist he gave his opinions frankly and freely, where the circumstances of his command, notably in the Baltic and the Mediterranean. obliged him to report to his Government the diplomatic negotiations which he had had to conduct; but though he never seems to have "posed" in the smallest degree as a statesman, the light since thrown on completed events shows how penetrating was his mind, and how correct his forecast.

Indeed, had his ideas and advice, in more than one instance, received the attention they are now proved to have merited, England herself, and in fact all Europe, might have been spared thousands of valuable lives and millions of treasure.

He predicted the movements of Buonaparte's troops in Italy, and had his despatches and advice been acted upon, England could beyond doubt have changed in an extraordinary degree, the then only threatened Dictatorship of France.

How the opinions formed on the spot, and the thoughtful counsels of so disinterested and single-minded a man as Nelson, could have been so often disregarded by his contemporaries, is difficult to comprehend, but so it was; still more difficult to understand, is the fact that the home authorities were so tardy in giving him anything like equivalent reward for his already long and unremitting services.

The dimensions of this book admitting only of an abridged enumeration of these earlier services, in order to devote a larger portion of space to the later, and greatest, events of his life, no better account can be found—although completely personal as it necessarily is—than that given by himself under the title of a " Sketch of my Life." After giving the date of his birth, and that he went to the High School at Norwich, and afterwards to North Walsham, he proceeds : —

"On the disturbance with Spain relative to the "Falkland Islands (in 1770), I went to sea with my "uncle, Captain Maurice Suckling, in the 'Raisonable,' "of 64 guns. But the business with Spain being "accommodated, I was sent in a West India ship "belonging to the house of Hibbert, Purrier & Horton, "with Mr. John Rathbone, who had formerly been in "the navy, in the 'Dreadnought' with Captain

" Suckling. From this voyage I returned to the
" ' Triumph ' at Chatham in July, 1772, and if I did not
" improve my education, I returned a practical seaman,
" with a horror of the Royal Navy, and with a saying,
" then constant with the seamen, 'aft the most honour,
" forward the better man.' It was many weeks before
" I got in the least reconciled to a man-of-war, so deep
" was the prejudice rooted ; and what pains were taken
" to instil this erroneous principle in a young mind!
" However, as my ambition was to be a seaman, it was
" always held out as a reward, that if I attended well
" to my navigation, I should go in a cutter and decked
" long-boat, which was attached to the commanding
" officer's ship at Chatham. Thus by degrees I
" became a good pilot, for vessels of that description,
" from Chatham to the Tower of London, down the
" Swin, and to the North Foreland ; and confident of
" myself amongst rocks and sands, which has many
" times since been of the very greatest comfort to me.
" In this way I was trained, till the expedition towards
" the North Pole was fitted out ; when, although no
" boys were allowed to go in the ships (as of no use),
" yet nothing could prevent my using every interest to
" go with Captain Lutwidge in the ' Carcass ;' and as I
" fancied I was to fill a man's place, I begged I might
" be his coxswain ; which, finding my ardent desire for
" going with him, Captain Lutwidge complied with, and
" has continued the strictest friendship to this moment.
" Lord Mulgrave, whom I then first knew, continued
" his kindest friendship and regard to the last moment
" of his life. When the boats were fitting out to quit
" the two ships blocked up in the ice, I exerted myself
" to have the command of a four-oared cutter raised
" upon, which was given me with twelve men, and I
" prided myself in fancying I could navigate her
" better than any other boat in the ship. On our
" arrival in England and paid off, 15th October (1773),

" I found that a squadron was fitting out for the East
" Indies, and nothing less than such a distant voyage
" could in the least satisfy my desire of maritime
" knowledge, and I was placed in the 'Seahorse,' of 20
" guns, with Captain Farmer, and watched in the
" foretop; from whence in time I was placed on the
" quarter-deck, having in the time I was in this ship
" visited almost every part of the East Indies, from
" Bengal to Bussorah.   Ill health induced Sir Edward
" Hughes, who had always shown me the greatest
" kindness, to send me to England in the 'Dolphin,' of
" 20 guns, with Captain James Pigot, whose kindness
" at that time saved my life.

   " This ship was paid off at Woolwich on 24th
" September, 1776.   On the 26th I received an order
" from Sir James Douglas, who commanded at Ports-
" mouth, to act as lieutenant of the 'Worcester,' 64,
" Captain Mark Robinson, who was ordered to
" Gibraltar with a convoy.   In this ship I was at sea
" with convoys till 2nd April, 1777, and in very bad
" weather.

   " But although my age might have been a sufficient
" cause for not entrusting me with the charge of a
" watch, yet Captain Robinson used to say, ' he felt as
" easy when I was upon deck as any officer in the ship.

   " On 9th April, 1777, I passed my examination as a
" lieutenant, and received my commission the next day,
" as second lieutenant of the 'Lowestoft,' frigate of 32
" guns, Captain (now Lieutenant-Governor of Green-
" wich Hospital) William Locker.   In this ship I went
" to Jamaica; but even a frigate was not sufficiently
" active for my mind, and I got into a schooner,[1] tender
" to the 'Lowestoft.'   In this vessel I made myself a
" complete pilot for all the passages through the (Keys)
" Islands situated on the north side of Hispaniola.

---

1 " The Little Lucy," so called after a daughter of Captain Locker.

" Whilst in this frigate an event happened which
" presaged my character; and, as it conveys no
" dishonour to the officer alluded to, I shall relate it.

" Blowing a gale of wind, and very heavy sea, the
" frigate captured an American letter of marque. The
" first lieutenant was ordered to board her, which he
" did not do, owing to the very high sea. On his return
" on board, the captain said, ' Have I no officer in the
" ship who can board the prize?' On which the
" master ran to the gangway to get into the boat;
" when I stopped him, saying, ' It is my turn now; and
" if I come back it is yours.' This little incident has
" often occurred to my mind; and I know it is my
" disposition that difficulties and dangers do but
" increase my desire of attempting them. Sir Peter
" Parker, soon after his arrival at Jamaica, 1778, took
" me into his own flag-ship, the ' Bristol,' as third
" lieutenant; from which I rose by succession to be
" first. Nothing particular happened whilst I was in
" this ship, which was actively employed off Cape
" François, being the commencement of the French
" war.

" On the 8th December, 1778, I was appointed com-
" mander of the ' Badger ' brig; and was first sent to
" protect the Mosquito shore and the Bay of
" Honduras from the depredations of the American
" privateers.

" Whilst on this service I gained so much the
" affections of the settlers that they unanimously voted
" me their thanks, and expressed their regret on my
" leaving them; entrusting me to describe to Sir Peter
" Parker and Sir John Dalling their situation, should a
" war with Spain break out. Whilst I commanded this
" brig, H.M.S. ' Glasgow,' Captain Thomas Lloyd,
" came into Montego Bay, Jamaica, where the ' Badger '
" was laying: in two hours afterwards she took fire by
" a cask of rum; and Captain Lloyd will tell you that

" it was owing to my exertions joined to his that her
'whole crew were rescued from the flames.

"On 11th June, 1779, I was made post into the
"'Hinchingbrook,' When, being at sea, and Count
'd'Estaing arriving at Hispaniola with a very large
fleet and army from Martinique, an attack on Jamaica
'was expected.

"In this critical state I was, by both Admiral and
'General, entrusted with the command of the batteries
'at Port Royal; and I need not say, as the defence of
' 'this place was the key to the port of the whole naval
' 'force, the town of Kingstown and Spanish Town, it
' 'was the most important post in the whole island.

"In January, 1780, an expedition being resolved on
' 'against St. Juan's, I was chosen to command the sea
' 'part of it. Major Polson, who commanded, will tell
' 'you of my exertions, how I quitted my ship, carried
' 'troops in boats 100 miles up a river, which none but
' 'Spaniards since the time of the buccaneers had ever
' 'ascended. It will then be told how I boarded, if I
" 'may be allowed the expression, an outpost of the
' 'enemy, situated on an island in the river; that I
' 'made batteries, and afterwards fought them, and was
' 'a principal cause of our success. From this scene I
" 'was appointed to the ' Janus,' 44, at Jamaica, and
' 'went to Port Royal in the ' Victor' sloop.

"My state of health was now so bad that I was
' 'obliged to go to England in the ' Lion,' the
' 'Honourable William Cornwallis, captain, whose care
' 'and attention again saved my life."

This autobiography is interrupted in order to add some
remarks Nelson wrote with regard to this deadly expedition.
After observing that had the expedition arrived at San
Juan's Harbour in January the violent torrents would have
subsided and the whole army would not have got wet three
or four times a day in dragging the boats, he continues : —

"The fever which destroyed the army and navy
" attached to that expedition was invariably from 20 to
" 30 days before it attacked the new-comers, and I
" cannot give a stronger instance than that in the
"'Hinchingbrook,' with a complement of 200 men, 87
" took to their beds in one night; and of the 200, 145
" were buried in mine and Captain Collingwood's time,
" and I believe very few, not more than ten, survived
" of that ship's crew—a proof how necessary expedition
" is in those climates."

To resume the autobiography :—

"In August, 1781, I was commissioned for the
"'Albemarle,' and it would almost be supposed, to try
" my constitution, was kept the whole winter in the
" North Sea.
    "In April, 1782, I sailed with a convoy for New-
" foundland and Quebec, under the orders of Captain
" Thomas Pringle.
    "From Quebec, during a cruise off Boston, I was
" chased by three French ships of the line, and the
"'Iris' frigate; as they all beat me in sailing very
" much, I had no chance left but running them
" amongst the shoals of St. George's Bank. This
" alarmed the line-of-battle ships, and they quitted the
" pursuit; but the frigate continued, and at sunset was.
" little more than gunshot distant, when, the line-of-
" battle ships being out of sight, I ordered the main-
" top sail to be laid to the mast, on this the frigate
" tacked, and stood to rejoin her consorts.
    " In October I sailed from Quebec with a convoy to
" New York, where I joined the fleet under the
" command of Lord Hood; and in November I sailed
" with him to the West Indies, where I remained till
" the peace, when I came to England, being directed in
" my way to attend H.R.H. the Duke of Clarence on

Nelson's Adventure with a Bear In 1773.

"November, I lived at Burnham Thorpe, County of
"Norfolk, in the parsonage house.

"In 1790, when the affair with Spain relative to
"Nootka Sound had near involved us in a war, I made
"use of every interest to get a ship, ay, even a boat, to
"serve my country, but in vain; there was a prejudice
"at the Admiralty evidently against me, which I can
"neither guess at nor in the least account for.

"On 30th January, 1793, I was commissioned in the
"very handsomest way for the 'Agamemnon,' 64, and
"was put under that great man and excellent officer,
"Lord Hood, appointed to the command in the
"Mediterranean."

That some prejudice existed against Nelson at the
Admiralty is tolerably certain, for he writes as late as May,
1795 (when he was about 36), to Captain Locker from the
Mediterranean.

"One hundred and ten days I have been actually
"engaged at sea and on shore against the enemy.
"Three actions against ships, two against Bastia, in my
"ship, four boat actions, and two villages taken, and 20
"sail of vessels burnt. I don't know anyone who has
"done more, and I have had the comfort to be ever
"applauded by my commander-in-chief, but never
"rewarded; and what is more mortifying, for services
"in which I have been slightly wounded, others have
"been praised who at the time were actually in bed, far
"from the scene of action."

In June, 1795, he writes to his brother, the Rev. William
Nelson.

"I have to boast, that no officer can this war, or any
"other that I know of, being in 15 months 110 days in
"action at sea and on shore."

In the execution of Admiral Hotham's orders to

co-operate with the Austrian General de Vins, in Vado
Bay, he came into action with a French Convoy in the
Bay of Alassia, and though his squadron was small

> "In less than one hour he cut out nine ships and
> "destroyed two others without the loss of a man
> "either killed or wounded."

In Admiral Hotham's official despatch it is said,

> "His officer-like conduct upon this, and indeed upon
> "every occasion when his services are called forth
> "reflects upon him the highest credit."

About this time some totally unfounded reports were
circulated by the Austrians, accusing the officers of the
English Fleet of conniving at the landing of supplies on the
Genoese coast by coasting vessels.

The letter which Nelson addressed on the subject to
Lord Grenville is a model of high-minded indignation that
such a report should have earned even the smallest
attention, and of the most unhesitating and courageous
assumption of responsibility, for after vindicating the
captains mentioned, he says : —

> "As this traitorous agreement could not be carried
> "on but by the consent of all captains, if they were on
> "the stations allotted to them, and as they could only
> "be drawn from these stations by orders from me, I
> "do most fully acquit all my brother captains from
> "such a combination, and have to request that I may
> "be considered as the only responsible person for
> "what is done under my command, if I approve of the
> "conduct of those under my orders, which in this most
> "public manner I beg to do ; for officers more alert,
> "and more anxious for the good and honour of their
> "King and country, can scarcely ever fall to the lot of
> "any commanding officer ; their names I place at the
> "bottom of this letter. For myself, from my earliest

"youth I have been in the naval service, and in two
"wars have been in more than 140 skirmishes and
"battles, at sea and on shore; have lost an eye, and
"otherwise blood, in fighting the enemies of my King
"and country; and God knows, instead of riches, my
"little fortune has been diminished in the service."

During the whole of his operations on the Genoese coast,
the squadron, already far too small at the beginning, was
reduced (under Sir Hyde Parker) to considerably less at
the end, and the condition of his own ship, the
"Agamemnon," was such, that when she was refitted at
Leghorn there was not a mast, yard, sail, or any of the
rigging which had not to be considerably repaired—all
damages from the shot that had hit her; and as to her hull,
that had for long been repaired by cables served round.

In 1796, the commander-in-chief, in recognition of his
services, desired Nelson to wear a distinguishing pendant, and he (Sir John Jervis) in a letter to Mr. Drake,
minister at Genoa, says :—

"I am happy to learn that Captain Nelson, whose
"zeal, activity, and enterprise cannot be surpassed,
"stands so high in your good opinion. I have only to
"lament the want of means to give him the command
"of a squadron equal to his merit."

That Sir John Jervis' good opinion of Nelson was fully
borne out, is evinced by the simple right-mindedness of the
following words, which occur in a letter to his wife written
at this time.

"As yet I appear to stand well with Sir John Jervis,
"and it shall not be my fault if I don't continue to do
"so. My conduct has no mystery. I freely communi-
"cate my knowledge and observations and only wish
"that whatever Admiral I serve under may make
"proper use of it. God forbid I should have any other
"consideration on service than the good of my country.

'. . .' Sir John Jervis by his manner, as I plainly
' perceive, does not wish me to leave this station. He
' seems at present to consider me more as an associate
' than a subordinate officer, for I am acting without
" orders. This may have its difficulties at a future
' day; but I make none, knowing the uprightness of
' my intentions. He asked me if I had heard any
' more of my promotion. I told him 'No.' His
" answer was, 'You must have a larger ship, for we
" cannot spare you either as captain or admiral.'"

Sir John Jervis wrote him a private letter saying:—

"No words can express the sense I entertain of
" every part of your conduct, and I shall be happy to
" manifest it in the most substantial manner; a
" distinguishing pendant you shall certainly wear, and
" I will write to Lord Spencer about you; in short,
" there is nothing within my grasp that I shall not be
" proud to confer on you."

From 1794, to June, 1796, Nelson's squadron had taken
in prizes 48 ships of various classes.

All the same, during the August of 1796, while writing of
returning home, in a long letter to his wife, he says:—

"God knows I shall come to you not a sixpence
" richer than when I set out."

And here it may be remarked that this requires no
corroboration, for he was well known always to be more
ready to give than to receive; and had he more actively
pushed his legitimate claims to substantial rewards, he
might have been a far richer man than he ever was. Up
to the time of the victorious Battle of the Nile he was a
really poor man, but even then he found means to give help
to many young officers, to send money to his father and his
family, and to the poor at home. The Treasury constantly
evaded the payment of his just claims, and refused to

remunerate him for his land services before Bastia and Calvi, or for the loss of his eye.

After the Battle of the Nile, the East India Company presented him with £10,000—and £2,000 of this he directly desired should be paid over to his father and family. Throughout his life, indeed, his money was given, and given often under difficulties, to those he considered needed it more than himself.

All the winter of 1796, Commodore Nelson was employed in the Mediterranean against the Fleet of Spain, as well as of France, the two countries having signed a treaty of alliance.

He was in various skirmishes more or less serious, used his invaluable influence at the evacuation of Corsica, and just before the English Fleet was ordered to Gibraltar in November, 1796, he was sent with two frigates to remove all the valuable stores at Porto Ferrajo.

His French biographer, Captain Jurien de la Gravière writes of this : —

> " He alone was capable of fulfilling this mission and
> " of penetrating fearlessly to the furthest part of the
> " Mediterranean, notwithstanding the squadrons that
> " were cruising about that vast sea, abandoned by
> " England to the united flags of France and Castile."

In December Nelson, on his way from Gibraltar, fell in with " La Santa Sabina " and " Ceres," off Cartagena, the result after a most severe action being that the Spanish ship, " La Sabina " (out of 286) lost 164 men, killed and wounded, and her captain, Don Jacobo Stuart (a descendant of James II.), gave up his sword to Nelson on the quarter-deck of " La Minerva." Nelson writes to his brother William : —

> " I hailed the Don . . . . I asked him
> " several times to surrender during the action, but his
> " answer was, ' No, sir, not whilst I have the means of

"fighting left!'   When only himself of all the officers
"was left alive, he hailed, and said he could fight no
"more, and begged me I would stop the firing."

On releasing Don Jacobo, Nelson wrote to the Spanish
admiral : —

{" Sir, I cannot allow **Don** Jacobo to return to you
"without expressing my admiration of his gallant
"conduct. . . . . I have endeavoured to make
"his captivity as easy as possible, and I rely on your
"generosity for reciprocal treatment towards my brave
"officers and men."

On St. Valentine's Day, 1797, was fought the great
battle of St. Vincent, in which Nelson's *anticipation* of
probable orders ensured the complete success of the British
fleet.

On this occasion Nelson has been accused of "disregard"
of orders, or that he corrected a tactical error of Sir John
Jervis ; but in reality it seems on later examination to have
been an anticipation of what he saw was absolutely
necessary, caused by a movement of the Spaniards, which
he had no time to communicate to Admiral Jervis, and he
therefore quitted his station without hesitating, and to his
movement was due the destruction of the enemy's ships,
and the victory was consequent upon his prompt action.

In the *Edinburgh Review* (1886), a critic writes : —

"The tactical error of Sir J. Jervis, which Nelson—
"terribly to his chief's humiliation—thus boldly
"corrected, had been the display of a wrong signal at
"a vital moment. Had Jervis made 'tack together' or
"'wear together,' instead of those which he did, the
"Spanish fleet would have been annihilated, for every
"English ship would then have turned round where
"she was, and would have brought her opponent to
"close action. Unquestionably Nelson would have
"used either of these signals, it did not require

" high intellectual effort, nor even genius. But it
" required singleness of mind and purpose—a clear
" vision of that which was immediately in view, and no
" thought of any kind beyond it."]

In reference to this battle, Mr. Lathom Browne, in his
" Life of Lord Nelson," writes : —

" Satisfied as Nelson was with the reception which
" he met with from Sir J. Jervis on the deck of the
" ' Victory,' he not unnaturally felt that his great
" service was overlooked in Sir John's official account
" of the victory.
" In that the only captain mentioned was Sir Robert
" Calder, 'whose able assistance,' wrote his chief,
" ' greatly contributed to the public service.'   Sir
" Robert, however, is less favourably known in history
" by his envious remark to Sir John ' that Nelson's act
" was that of disobedience to orders,' and the rebuff he
" met with, ' I saw it, but if ever you commit such a
" breach of orders, I will forgive you also.'   It will be
" seen how before the day of Trafalgar Nelson did his
" best—even at the cost of weakening his fleet—to
" enable Calder to obtain witnesses in his own favour,
" and proceed without delay to England to meet the
" charge that lay against him of not having done his
" duty in his engagement with the allied fleet.
" Jealousy of his professional brethren was unknown to
" Nelson."

On the morning after the action of St. Vincent, Nelson
wrote to Captain Collingwood : —

" My dearest friend, a friend in need is a friend
" indeed,' was never more truly verified than by your
" most noble and gallant conduct yesterday in sparing
" the ' Captain ' from further loss ; and I beg, both as
" a public officer and a friend, you will accept my most

"sincere thanks. I have not failed by letter to the
"Admiral to represent the services of the ' Excellent.' "

The account is well known of Nelson's boarding the
Spanish "first-rate," and on his getting into her main
chains, how a Spanish officer unarmed came and said she
surrendered, and how on her quarter-deck Nelson received
the swords of all the vanquished Spaniards, which he gave
over to William Fearney, one of his bargemen, "who
placed them with the greatest *sang froid* under his arm."
He himself writes : —

"The 'Victory' passing saluted us with three cheers,
"as did every ship in the fleet."

For this victory Sir J. Jervis was made Earl St. Vincent,
and Nelson was given the Order of the Bath, which was the
honour he most desired.

In the blockading in Cadiz of the "fugitive Spanish
squadron," Nelson was actively engaged.

He had hoisted his flag on the "Theseus," and on the
first attempt of the Spanish fleet to get out of harbour they
had 28 sail-of-the-line and a considerable number of large
armed launches and mortar gunboats.

Nelson's attack on them, however, was so swift and
determined that they gave way in great confusion, and took
refuge under their own guns. Nelson in this fight was in
continual danger, as he, Captain Fremantle, and his own
ten bargemen were engaged in a hand to hand struggle
with 26 men in an armed Spanish launch.

In this encounter—

"His faithful follower, John Sykes, twice saved
"Nelson's life by parrying blows that were aimed at
"him, and at last actually interposed his own head to
"receive the blows of a Spanish sabre, which he could
"not by any other means avert."

Had his length of service been sufficient Nelson would
have endeavoured to get him made a lieutenant.

Sykes recovered from his wound, but did not live long enough for promotion.

That John Sykes was not singular in his devotion, is proved by a paper having been dropped on the " Theseus " quarter-deck about a fortnight before, with these words : —

> " Success attend Admiral Nelson! God bless
> " Captain Miller! We thank them for the officers they
> " have placed over us. We are happy and comfortable,
> " and will shed every drop of blood in our veins to
> " support them, and the name of the ' Theseus ' shall
> " be immortalized as high as the ' Captain's ' ship's
> " company."

On the 21st of July, 1797, Nelson made his first attempt to take the town of Santa Cruz ; a venture he had thought out for some time before, but which he was now forced to undertake with serious difficulty, owing to the Military Commander not considering his orders would allow him to co-operate with the naval forces.

However, Nelson made the first attempt with four line-of-battle ships, three frigates, and the " Fox " cutter.

The log of the " Theseus " gives an account which clearly shows the desperate nature of the expedition.

> " Captains Troubridge, Hood, Miller, and Waller,
> " landed with part of the boats, just to the Southward
> " of the Citadel, passing through a raging surf which
> " stove all the boats and wet all the ammunition.
> " Notwithstanding these difficulties, they pushed over
> " the enemy's line wall and batteries, and formed in the
> " great square of the town, about 80 marines, 80
> " pikemen, and 180 small-armed seamen (total 340),
> " where they took possession of a convent, from
> " whence they marched against the citadel, but found
> " it far beyond their power to take. At daylight, from
> " prisoners taken, Captain Troubridge found there were
> " 8,000 Spaniards in arms, and 100 French, with five

" field pieces, assembled at the entrance of the town,
" and seeing the impossibility of getting any assistance
" from the ships, at seven o'clock he sent Captain Hood
" with a message to the governor, that if he should be
" allowed, freely and without molestation to embark
" his people at the mole head, taking off such boats as
" were not stove, and that the Governor should find
" others to carry off the people, the squadron before the
" town would not molest it.

" The Governor told Captain Hood he thought they
" ought to surrender as prisoners of war, to which he
" replied that Captain Troubridge had directed him to
" say that if the terms he had offered were not accepted
" in five minutes, he would set the town on fire and
" attack the Spaniards at the point of the bayonet, on
" which the Governor instantly closed with the terms,
" when Captain Troubridge marched with British
" colours flying to the mole, where they embarked in
" such of our boats as were not stove, the Spaniards
" finding others to carry them to their ships."

The Spanish Governor, Don Juan Antonio Gutierres,
behaved nobly and generously as soon as the terms were
agreed on, as he directed that all our wounded men should
be received into the hospitals, and our people be supplied
with the best available provisions, our ships also being
allowed to send on shore for what they wanted.

After his only partial success on the 23rd, Nelson wrote
to his chief, announcing his intention to recommence the
attack on the morrow, and, should he fall, recommending
his step-son to the Admiral and to his country. This is
supposed to be the last letter he wrote with his right hand.
On the morrow Southey records : —

" Perfectly aware how desperate a service this was
" likely to prove, before he left the ' Theseus ' he
" called Lieutenant Nisbet . . . perceiving that the
" young man was armed, he earnestly begged him to

"remain behind. 'Should we both fall, Josiah,' said
"he, 'what would become of your poor mother? The
"care of the 'Theseus' falls to you, stay therefore and
"take charge of her.' Nisbet replied, 'Sir, the ship
"must take care of herself; I will go with you to-night,
"if I never go again.' . . . . In act of stepping
"out of the boat Nelson received a shot through the
"right elbow and fell; but as he fell he caught the
"sword which he had just drawn in his left hand,
"determined never to part with it while he lived, for it
"had belonged to his uncle, Captain Suckling, and he
"valued it like a relic. Nisbet, who was close to him,
"placed him at the bottom of the boat, and laid his hat
"over the shattered arm, lest the sight of the blood,
"which gushed out in great abundance, should increase
"his faintness. He then examined the wound, and
"taking some silk handkerchiefs from his neck, bound
"them tightly over the lacerated vessels.

"One of his bargemen, Lovel, tore his shirt into
"shreds and made a sling with them for the broken
"limb.

"They then collected five other seamen, by whose
"assistance they succeeded at length in getting the
"boat afloat, for it had grounded with the falling tide.
"Nisbet took one of the oars, and ordered the
"steersman to go close under the guns of the battery,
"that they might be safe from the tremendous fire.
"Hearing his voice Nelson roused himself and desired
"to be lifted up that he might look about him.
"Nisbet raised him up, but nothing could be seen
"except the firing of the guns on shore, and what
'could be discerned by their flashes upon the stormy
'sea. In a few minutes a general shriek was heard
'from the crew of the 'Fox,' which had received a
shot under water and went down. 97 men were lost
in her; 83 were saved, many by Nelson himself,
whose exertions on this occasion greatly increased

" the pain and danger of his wound. The first ship
" which the boat could reach was the ' Seahorse,' but
" nothing could induce him to go on board, though he
" was assured that if they attempted to row to another
" ship it might be at the risk of his life. ' I had rather
" suffer death,' he replied, ' than alarm Mrs. Fremantle
" by letting her see me in this state, when I can give
" her no tidings whatever of her husband.' They
" pushed on for the ' Theseus,' when they came along-
" side he peremptorily refused all assistance in getting
" on board, so impatient was he that the boat should
" return in hopes that it might save a few more from
" the ' Fox.' He desired to have only a single rope
" thrown over the side which he twisted round his left
" hand, saying, ' Let me alone ! I have yet my legs and
" one arm, tell the surgeon to hasten and get his
" instruments. I know I must lose my right arm ; so
" the sooner it is off the better.' The spirit he
" displayed in jumping up the ship's side astonished
" everybody."

Mr. Lathom Browne says : —

    " Such was Nelson ever, no thought about himself,
" every thought for others."

In his despatch he did not mention his severe wound,
but on the 27th of July he wrote the following letter, the
first with his left hand, to Sir J. Jervis, and it shows how
fully the bravery with which he had borne the wound was
equalled by the bitterness with which he felt his loss.

    " My dear sir, I am become a burden to my friends
" and useless to my country, but by my letter of the
" 24th you will perceive my anxiety for the promotion
" of my son-in-law (stepson) Josiah Nisbet. When I
" leave your command I become dead to the world ; I
" go hence and am no more seen. If from poor
" Bowen's loss you think proper to oblige me, I rest

" confident you will do it ; the boy is under obligations
" to me, but he repaid me by bringing me from the
" mole of Santa Cruz. I hope you will be able to give
" me a frigate to convey the remains of my carcase to
" England. God bless you, my dear sir, and believe
" me, &c.,

"HORATIO NELSON.

" You will excuse this scrawl, considering it is my first
" attempt."

On August 10th he says in a second letter : —

" A left-handed Admiral will never again be
" considered useful ; therefore the sooner I get to my
" very humble cottage the better to make room for a
" better man to serve the state, but whatsoever be my
" lot, believe me, with the most sincere affection, ever
" your most faithful,

" H. N."

Nelson arrived in England on September 1st, and went
to Bath and thence to London, suffering for three months
almost constant pain, his wife dressing the wounded arm—
which would not heal until the silk ligature which had
become fast to the nerve came away. It is related that : —

" One night during this state of acute suffering when
" Nelson was lodging in Bond Street, and had retired
" early to bed in the hope of getting some rest from
" laudanum, the love and respect felt for him was
" shown by the crowd, who were calling on all persons
" to illuminate for Duncan's victory at Camperdown.
" When they were told that Nelson lay there in bed
" the foremost of them replied, ' you shall hear no more
" of us to night.' The word was passed from crowd to
" crowd, and the house was not molested again."

He received an extremely kind letter from H.R.H. the
Duke of Clarence, to which he returned the following
answer :—

" Sir, I trust your Royal Highness will attribute my
" not having sent a letter since my arrival to its true
" cause—viz: the not being now a ready writer. I
" feel confident of your sorrow for my accident, but I
" assure your Royal Highness that not a scrap of that
" ardour with which I have served our King has been
" shot away."

Before he could receive the pension proposed to be given
him of £1,000 a year, he was obliged to send to the King a
memorial enumerating his services, and we find them thus
detailed : —

" That during the present war your memorialist has
" been in four actions with the fleets of the enemy, viz.,
" on the 13th and 14th of March, 1795, on the 13th of
" July, and on the 14th of February, 1797, in three
" actions with frigates, in six engagements against
" batteries, in ten actions in boats in cutting out of
" harbours, in destroying vessels, and in taking three
" towns. Your memorialist has also served on shore
" with the army four months, and commanded the
" batteries at the sieges of Bastia and Calvi. That
" during the war he has assisted at the capture of seven
" sail-of-the-line, six frigates, four corvettes, and eleven
" privateers of different sizes, and destroyed near 50
" sail of merchant vessels ; and your memorialist has
" actually been engaged against the enemy upwards of
" 150 times. In which service your memorialist has
" lost his right eye and arm, and been severely
" wounded and bruised in his body."

On his restoration to health he sent this request to the
clergyman of the parish church : —

" An officer desires to return thanks to Almighty
" God for his perfect recovery from a severe wound,
" and also for the many mercies bestowed upon him
" (for next Sunday), December 8th, 1797."

On that date also he writes to Captain Berry :—

> " If you mean to marry, I would recommend your
> " doing it speedily, or the to-be Mrs. Berry will have
> " very little of your company ; for I am well, and you
> " may expect to be called for every hour."

We find in his autobiography : —

> " On the 19th of December, 1797, the ' Vanguard '
> " was commissioned for my flag-ship. On the 1st of
> " April, 1798, I sailed with a convoy from Spithead.
> " I joined Earl St. Vincent off Cadiz on April 29th."

At the same time the news reached Lord St. Vincent
from the British Consul at Leghorn, that there were
already nearly 400 sail of French vessels in the Mediterranean harbours of France and Italy. The danger was
that these ships, with others as escort, could transport
40,000 soldiers to Sicily, Malta, or elsewhere, and it was
this information which first threw light on Buonaparte's
probable designs for the acquisition of Egypt, and for the
control of our high road to India.

Lord St. Vincent at once sent the " Vanguard," " Orion,"
and " Alexander," four frigates, and a corvette, under the
command of Nelson, to cruise about and watch the French.
Lord Spencer wrote privately from home to the Admiral,
saying : —

> " If you determine to send a detachment, I think it
> " almost unnecessary to suggest to you the propriety
> " of putting it under the command of Sir H. Nelson,
> " whose acquaintance with that part of the world, as
> " well as his activity and disposition, seem to qualify
> " him in a peculiar manner for that service."

Great opposition was made to his appointment by his
senior officers. Lord St. Vincent wrote to him on June
22nd : —

Rear-Admiral Nelson's Conflict with a Spanish Launch.
July 3rd, 1797.

" secret of the expedition had been well kept.   .   .
" Amidst so many suppositions Nelson could only rely
" on his own judgment, and it must be admitted that in
" tracking the French squadron, he showed from the
" first as much sagacity as activity."

In this search, however, fortune was against him, for
finding the harbour at Alexandria empty, he started at once
on his return to Sicily, and being forced to beat against
contrary winds he just missed sight of the French through
tacking beyond the track of their squadron.

He asked permission to water his fleet at Syracuse, and
left again forthwith in search of the enemy.   During all
these days he occupied his time in consulting his captains,
his " Band of Brothers " as he called them, as to the best
plans to adopt, and Captain Berry writes : —

" The Admiral had, and it appeared most justly,
" the highest opinion of, and placed the firmest reliance
" on, the valour and conduct of every captain in his
" squadron.   It had been his practice .   .   .   .   . to
" have his captains on board the ' Vanguard,' where he
" would develop to them his own ideas of the different
" and best modes of attack, and such plans as he
" proposed to execute upon falling in with the enemy,
" whatever their situation or position might be, by day
" or by night.   .   .   .   .   With the masterly ideas of
" their Admiral, therefore, on the subject of naval
" tactics, every one of the captains of his squadron was
" most thoroughly acquainted.   .   .   .   .   We saw
" the Pharos of Alexandria at noon on the 1st of
" August (1798).   .   .   .   .   The enemy's fleet was
" first discovered by Captain Hood, who immediately
" communicated by signal the number of ships, 16,
" lying at anchor in line-of-battle in a bay on the
" larboard bow, which was afterwards discovered to be
" Aboukir Bay.   The Admiral hauled his wind that

C

" instant, a movement . . . followed by the whole
" squadron. . . . . He made signal to prepare for
" battle. . . . . The position of the enemy pre-
" sented the most formidable obstacles; but the
" Admiral viewed these with the eye of a seaman
" determined on attack, and it instantly struck his
" eager and penetrating eye, *that where there was*
" *room for an enemy's ship to swing, there was room*
" *for one of ours to anchor.* No further signal was
" necessary. . . . . The Admiral's designs were
" as fully known to his whole squadron as was his
" determination to conquer or perish in the attempt."

The Battle of the Nile commenced about half-past six,
by seven o'clock it was quite dark, and all the ships were
obliged to hoist signal lights, and by half-past eight
the vanship " Le Guerrier," the " Conquerant," " Le
Spartiate," " L'Aquilon," and " Le Peuple Souverain," all
surrendered or were taken.

At that hour Lieutenant Galway of the " Vanguard " was
sent with a party of marines to take possession of " Le
Spartiate," and returning with the French captain's sword
immediately delivered it to the admiral, who was below in
consequence of a severe wound he had received in the head
during the heat of the attack. It appeared the victory was
then ours, although " L'Orient," " L'Heureux," and " Le
Tonnant " were not taken, but they were considered in our
power. At a few minutes past nine a fire broke out on
board the French flag-ship " L'Orient," and burning with
great rapidity soon enveloped half the ship in flames.

Nelson, in spite of his wound, immediately came up on
deck, and his first thought was to save as many lives as
possible. He ordered Captain Berry to make every
exertion to do so, and in consequence about 70 Frenchmen
were saved.

" The cannonading was partially kept up to leeward

" of the centre till about ten o'clock, when ' L'Orient '
" blew up with a tremendous explosion.

" An awful pause and death-like silence for about
" three minutes ensued, when the wreck of the masts,
" yards, etc., which had been carried to a vast height,
" fell down into the water, and on board the surround-
" ing ships. . . . . After this awful scene, the
" firing was re-commenced with the ships to leeward of
" the centre, till twenty minutes past ten, when there
" was a total cessation of firing for about ten minutes,
" after which it was revived till about three in the
" morning, when it again ceased."

Nelson wrote to Lord St. Vincent on the 2nd August :—

" My Lord, Almighty God has blessed His Majesty's
" arms in the late battle by a great victory over the
" fleet of the enemy, whom I attacked at sunset on the
" 1st of August in a strong line of battle for defending
" the entrance of the Bay (of shoals), flanked by
" numerous gunboats, four frigates, and a battery of
" guns and mortars on an island in their van ; but
" nothing could withstand the squadron your lordship
" did me the honour to place under my command.
" Their high state of discipline is well known to you,
" and with the judgment of the captains, together with
" their valour, and that of the officers and men of every
" description, it was absolutely irresistible. Could
" anything more from my pen add to the character of
" the captains, I would write it with pleasure. . . .
" The support and assistance I have received from
" Captain Berry cannot be sufficiently expressed. I
" was wounded in the head and obliged to be carried
" off the deck ; but the service suffered no loss by
" that event."

Buonaparte's despatches were taken in this action, and
the Admiral learnt therein of his " intention " to " take Suez

and Damietta," and also that he was in distress for stores, artillery, etc. Nelson writes :—

> " You may be assured I shall remain here as long as
> " possible. Buonaparte had never yet to contend with
> " an English officer, and I shall make him respect us."

His autobiography continues :—

> " On the 22nd of September, 1798, I arrived at
> " Naples and was received by the king, queen, and the
> " whole kingdom.
> " October 12th, the blockade of Malta took place,
> " which has continued without intermission to this day
> " (October 13th, 1700).
> " On the 21st December, 1798, his Sicilian majesty
> " and family embarked in the ' Vanguard,' and were
> " carried to Palermo, in Sicily.
> " In March, 1799, I arranged a plan for taking the
> " Islands in the Bay of Naples, and for supporting the
> " Royalists, who were making head in the kingdom.
> " This plan succeeded in every part. In May I
> " shifted my flag, being promoted to be Rear-Admiral
> " of the Red, to the ' Foudroyant' and was obliged to
> " be on my guard against the French Fleet.
> " In June and July, 1799, I went to Naples, and, as
> " his Sicilian Majesty is pleased to say, reconquered
> " his kingdom and placed him on his throne.
> " On the 19th of August I brought back his Sicilian
> " Majesty to Palermo, having been upwards of four
> " weeks on board the ' Foudroyant.'
> " On the 13th his Sicilian Majesty presented me
> " with a sword, magnificently enriched with diamonds,
> " the title of Duke of Bronte, and annexed to it the
> " feud of Bronte, supposed to be worth £3,000 per
> " annum.
> " On the arrival of the Russian Squadron at Naples
> " I directed Commodore Troubridge to go with the

"Squadron, and blockade closely Civita Vecchia, and
"to offer to the French most favourable conditions if
"they would evacuate Rome and Civita Vecchia;
"which the French General, Grenier, complied with,
"and they were signed on board the 'Culloden' when
"a prophecy, made to me on my arrival at Naples, was
"fulfilled, viz., *that I should take Rome with my*
"*Ships.'*

"Thus may be exemplified by my Life that perse-
"verance in my profession will most probably meet its
"reward. Without having any inheritance, or being
"fortunate in prize money, I have received all the
"honours of my profession, been created a Peer c!
"Great Britain, and I may say to thee, reader :

"'Go thou and do likewise.'

"NELSON.

"October 15th, 1799,
"Port Mahon."

That here should have ended Nelson's Autobiography is
ever to be deplored, for had it been continued it would
doubtless have made impossible most of the invented and
regrettable gossip and misunderstandings, which have far
too long been allowed to cling around his great name.

Happily, however, within the last few years, several
authors have published—as the result of their critical
researches—details and opinions so far more consistent
with his whole character and career, that a reference to
their works should finally dispose of the errors contained in
Southey's work, and in those others compiled with less
adherence to truth than was his.

The enthusiasm and excitement with which he was
welcomed at Naples, though passed over in his official
despatch, are partially described to his wife in several
letters. In the first he writes :—

"The poor wretched 'Vanguard' arrived here on
"the 22nd of September.

" I must endeavour to convey to you something of
" what passed ; but if it was so affecting to those who
" were only united to me by bonds of friendship, what
" must it be to my dearest wife, my friend, my every-
" thing which is .most dear to me in this world ? Sir
" William and Lady Hamilton came out to sea, attended
" by numerous boats, with emblems, etc.

" They, my most respectable friends, had really been
" laid up and seriously ill, first from anxiety, and then
" from joy. It was imprudently told Lady Hamilton
" in a moment, and the effect was like a shot ; she fell
" apparently dead, and is not yet perfectly recovered
" from severe bruises.

" Alongside came my honoured friends. . . .
" Tears, however, soon set matters to rights, when
" alongside came the King. . . . He took me by
" the hand, calling me his 'Deliverer and Preserver,'
" with every other expression of kindness.

" In short all Naples calls me ' Nostro Liberatore ;'
" my greeting from the lower classes was truly
" affecting.

" I hope some day to have the pleasure of intro-
" ducing you to Lady Hamilton ; she is one of the best.
" women in this world ; she is an honour to her sex.
" Her kindness, with Sir William's, to me is more than
" I can express ; I am in their house, and I may tell
" you that it required all the kindness of my friends to
" set me up.

" Lady Hamilton intends writing to you. May God
" Almighty bless you, and give us in due time a happy
" meeting.

" H. N."

At the moment of his arrival at Naples he was barely
recovering from an attack of fever, his life having been
despaired of for eighteen hours, and he was still—he wrote
to Lord St. Vincent—

" very weak in body and mind from my cough and this
" fever.

"I never expect, my lord, to see your face again ; it
" may please God that this battle will be the finish of
" that fever of anxiety which I have endured from the
" middle of June ; but be that as it pleases His good-
" ness, I am resigned to His will."

He tells Lady Nelson, in a letter dated September 28th,
1798 : —

"The preparations of Lady Hamilton for cele-
" brating my birthday to-morrow are enough to fill me
" with vanity.   Every ribbon, every button, has
" Nelson, etc.   The whole service is marked 'H. N.,
" glorious 1st of August.' Songs and sonetti· are
" numerous beyond what I ever could deserve.

"I send the additional verse to 'God save the
" King,' as I know you will sing it with pleasure.
" .   .   .   .

"The Queen yesterday, being still ill, sent her
" favourite son to visit and bring me a letter from her
" of gratitude and thanks. . .   All glory be to God!
" The more I think, the more I hear, the greater is my
" astonishment at the extent and good consequences of
" our victory."

The additional verse to the National Anthem was written
by Miss Cornelia Knight, and ran thus : —

> Join we in great Nelson's name
> First on the rolls of fame ;
>   Him let us sing.
> Spread we his fame around,
> Honour of British ground,
> Who made Nile's shore resound,
>   God save the King.

From October 1st to the 6th he writes to his wife : —

" Our time here is actively employed and, between

" business and what is called pleasure, I am not my
" own master for five minutes. The combined kind
" attention of Sir W. and Lady Hamilton must ever
" make you and I love them, they are deserving of the
" admiration of all the world. The grand signor has
" ordered me a valuable diamond. If it were worth a
" million my pleasure would be to see it in your
" possession. My pride is being your husband, the
" son of my dear father, and in having Sir William and
" Lady Hamilton for my friends.

  " Could I, my dearest Fanny, tell you half the
" honours which are shown me here, not a ream of
" paper would hold it.

  " On my birthday 80 people dined at Sir William
" Hamilton's and 1,740 came to a ball."

The victory of the Nile had a great and immediate
influence on European feeling and politics, with regard to
France ; Austria and Russia especially desiring to join
England actively against France.

If Nelson could have followed up his own ideas and
advice, the French army in Egypt would almost certainly
have become his prisoners of war.

Austria declared war, Russia prepared to do so, and the
King of Naples yielding to Nelson's advice, joined the
three powers with 80,000 men under General Mack, of
whom, however, Nelson had no very high opinion.

How far incapacity or the treachery of other officers
was to blame is uncertain, but, for the moment, the
Neapolitan cause was lost. In a letter of December 11th,
1798, to Lord Spencer, Nelson says : —

  " The Neapolitan officers have not lost much honour,
" for God knows they had but little to lose, but they
" lost all they had. Mack has supplicated the King to
" sabre every man who ran from Civita Castellana to
" Rome."

He then proceeds to detail the position of the Neapolitan army, the right wing of 19,000 men of which had been sent to take post between Ancona and Rome to cut off supplies and communication. Near Fermi they met the French enemy numbering about 3,000.

Their General, St. Philip, thereon went over to the French, the other General, Michaux, ran away, as did all the Infantry, and they were only saved by the good conduct of two Regiments of Cavalry.

"So great was their panic that cannon, tents, "baggage, and military chests, all were left to the "French."

The Neapolitans lost only 40 men, but the—

"Peasantry took up arms, even the women, to "defend their country."

General Mack in a subsequent action was severely wounded, having been deserted by his own men, when again some Cavalry came to the rescue.

In the meantime Nelson had taken all the active measures he could for the firmer blockade of Malta, and for the capture of Leghorn, and had then returned to Naples.

Day by day the condition of the Royal Family became more insecure, and finally on the 21st of December the whole of the Royal Family, with the British Minister, Sir W. Hamilton, and his wife, went at night on board the "Vanguard," and Nelson sailed with them for Sicily and landed them at Palermo.

For six months Nelson guarded the Royal Family, only leaving the Sicilian coast when obliged to do so through the rumoured escape of a French squadron from Brest, and when he returned to Naples.

He there found anarchy and rebellion still, but after many difficulties Nelson, by his firm and straightforward

conduct of affairs, gained the day, conquered the
insurgents, ordered them to surrender to His Majesty's
Royal mercy and took possession of the Castles of Uovo
and Nuovo, which had been seized by the rebels and
garrisoned by the French.

In July, 1799, Malta was still in the hands of the French,
through the neglect and insufficiency of the English
General, and an expedition to Minorca could not be carried
out for want of money.

> "The cause cannot stand still for want of a little
> "money (said Nelson), if nobody will pay it I will sell
> "Bronte and the Emperor of Russia's box."

In the end, however, the expedition set out, and on his
way to Malta Nelson encountered " Le Généreux," which
vessel had barely escaped capture at the battle of the Nile,
and she surrendered after a short, but sharp, engagement.
This was in February, 1800, and on March 30th following,
Sir Edward Berry writes to Nelson : —

> "After a most gallant defence 'Le Guillaume Tell'
> "surrendered.   She is completely dismasted, . . .
> "all hands behaved as you could have wished. How
> "we prayed for you, God knows, and your sincere and
> "faithful friend,
>
>   "E. BERRY."

This left two frigates only, which had escaped out of all
the French vessels engaged in the action of the Nile, and
of these one was afterwards taken.

Showing how Nelson delighted to honour his brother
officers we may quote part of his official letter to the
Admiralty on this capture.

> "The 'Lion' and the 'Foudroyant' lost each 40
> "killed and wounded; the French ship is dismasted;
> "the French Admiral Decrès wounded; the 'Foud-
> "royant' much shattered. I send Sir E. Berry's hasty
> "note.

" Thus, owing to my brave friends, is the entire
" capture and destruction of the French Mediterranean
" Fleet to be attributed, and my orders from the great
" Earl St. Vincent fulfilled.   Captain Blackwood of
" the ' Penelope,' and Captain Long of the ' Vincejo,'
" have the greatest merit. . . ."

After conveying the Queen of Naples and her family to
Léghorn, he struck his flag on the 13th of July and shortly
left for England, accompanied by Sir W. and Lady
Hamilton, and as far as Vienna they travelled with the
Queen of Naples, who had decided on going thither. Viâ
Prague, Dresden, and Hamburg, they arrived in England,
and landed at Yarmouth on the 6th of November, where
Nelson was received with a warmth of welcome commen-
surate with his great deeds.

Everywhere his presence evoked the greatest enthusiasm; he was presented with a sword by the City of
London, the people taking the horses from his carriage,
and dragging it through the cheering crowd from Ludgate
Hill to the Guildhall.

Public visits to the theatres, dinners given in his honour
followed, and on the 20th of November, 1800, Lord Nelson
took his seat in the House of Lords.

During the early part of the year 1801, various disagree-
ments which had arisen between the Northern Powers of
Europe and the English Government had become serious
enough to necessitate the preparation of the Baltic
Expedition, and in February of that year Nelson hoisted
his flag on board the " St. George," under Sir Hyde Parker.

He sailed in this squadron through a strong sense of
duty, for he was confessedly both uneasy and unhappy, as
he could not help fretting under delays he judged rightly
were both needless and unadvisable, and he very naturally
chafed at being obliged to obey—as he did obey in the
most complete manner—a commander-in-chief who was
second to himself in every possible respect but that of

service seniority. Nevertheless, he ends a long service letter to Sir Hyde, in which he places before him his own counsels on the coming battle of Copenhagen, with these words : —

"In supporting you, my dear Sir Hyde, through the "arduous and important task you have undertaken, no "exertion of head or heart shall be wanting from your "most obedient and faithful servant,

"NELSON AND BRONTE."

The natural difficulties and dangers of the passages between the German Ocean and the Baltic were very great, the defences the Danes had had time to construct—serious obstacles.

The commander-in-chief tried one passage, turned back and anchored, held consultations with his officers, at one of which Nelson exclaimed, "I don't care by which passage we go, so that we fight them!" and it was only on the fourth day that the fleet started.

Nelson wrote to Captain Troubridge : —

"March 30th, 6 o'clock in the morning. We are "now standing for Cronenberg ; the van is formed in a "compact line, and old Stricker, for that is the "Governor's name, had better take care we don't "strike his head off.

"I hope we shall mend on board the 'London,' but "I now pity Sir Hyde and Domet (Flag Captain), they "both, I fancy, wish themselves elsewhere. You may "depend on every exertion of mine to keep up "harmony. For the rest, the spirit of the fleet will "make all difficulty from enemies appear as nothing. "I do not think I ever saw more true a desire to "distinguish themselves in my life. I have more to tell "you if ever we meet . . . . . Ever your "affectionate,

"NELSON AND BRONTE."

The Battle of Copenhagen was fought on the 2nd of April, 1801, and on the 3rd Nelson reports to Sir H. Parker, that through the able assistance of Captains Rion and Brisbane and the Masters of the "Amazon" and "Cruiser" in particular, the squadron passed in safety, and he—

> "Engaged the Danish line, consisting of six sail-of-
> "the-line, eleven floating batteries, mounting from 26
> "twenty-four pounders to 18 eighteen-pounders, and
> "one bomb ship, besides schooner gun-vessels. These
> "were supported by the Crown Islands, mounting 88
> "cannon, and four sail-of-the-line moored in the
> "harbour's mouth, and some batteries on the Island of
> "Anak The bomb ship and schooner gun-vessels
> "made their escape. The other 17 sail are sunk,
> "burnt, or taken, being the whole of the Danish line
> "to the southward of the Crown Islands, after a battle
> "of four hours. From the very intricate navigation
> "the 'Bellona' and 'Russell' unfortunately grounded.
> ".   .   .   .   The 'Agamemnon' could not weather the
> "shoals of the middle ground, and was obliged to
> "anchor, but not the smallest blame can be attached
> "to Captain Faircourt."

Nelson had shifted his flag to the "Elephant," a smaller vessel, and had led the van. He had personally superintended the soundings to be taken, and the surgeon of the "Elephant" has put this on record, for he has written :—

> "I could only admire, when I saw the first man in all
> "the world spend the hours of the day and night in the
> "boats, and wonder, when the light showed me a path
> "marked by buoys, which was trackless the preceding
> "evening."

The many despatches and accounts of this period are far too voluminous to quote here, but we may add the story

told by Colonel Stewart of Nelson's "disregard" of the
Admiral's signal.   Colonel Stewart recounts :—

"About one p.m., when the contest in general,
"though from the relaxed state of the enemy's fire it
"might not have given much room for apprehension
"as to the result, had not declared itself on either side,
"Sir Hyde Parker made 'Signal No. 30.' Lord
"Nelson was at this time, as he had been during the
"whole action, walking the starboard side of the
"quarter-deck; sometimes much animated, at others
"heroically fine in his observations.   A shot through
"the mainmast knocked a few splinters about us.   He
"observed to me with a smile, 'It is warm work, and
"this day may be the last of any of us at a moment;'
"and then, stopping short at the gangway, he used an
"expression never to be erased from my memory, and
"said with emotion, 'I would not be elsewhere for
"thousands.'   When the signal No. 30 (cease firing)
"was made, the signal lieutenant reported it to him.
"He continued his walk, and did not appear to take
"notice of it.   The lieutenant meeting his lordship at
"the next turn, asked 'whether he should repeat it?'
"Lord Nelson answered, 'No, acknowledge it.'   On
"the officer returning to the poop, his Lordship called
"after him, 'Is No. 16 still hoisted?'   The lieutenant
"answering in the affirmative, Lord Nelson said,
"'Mind you keep it so!'   He now walked the deck
"considerably agitated, which was always known by
"his moving the stump of his right arm.   After a turn
"or two, he said to me in a quick manner, 'Do you
"know what's shown on board the Commander-in-
"Chief, No. 30?'   On asking him what that meant, he
"answered, 'Why, to leave off action.'   'Leave off
"action,' he repeated, and then added with a shrug,
"'Now, damn me if I do!'
"He also observed I believe, to Captain Foley, 'I

"have only one eye—I have a right to be blind some-
"times,' and then with an archness peculiar to his
"character, putting the glasses to his blind eye, he
"exclaimed, 'I really do not see the signal.'"

Whatever motive the Commander-in-Chief had for
hoisting this signal at such a moment will now never be
known with absolute certainty, but the balance of opinion
is said to incline towards the following explanation given in
the biography of the Rev. A. Scott, Nelson's chaplain, and
also his devoted friend—

"The simple version of this circumstance is, that
"it had been arranged between the Admirals, that if
"it should appear that the ships which were engaged
"were suffering too severely, the signal for retreat
"should be made, to give Lord Nelson the option of
"retiring, if he thought fit."

The Danes fought well, but after the victory was decided
they persisted in firing on our boats as we took possession
of the ships which had struck, and at last Nelson wrote the
following letter to the Crown Prince.

"To the brothers of Englishmen, the Danes.

"Lord Nelson has directions to spare Denmark, when
"no longer resisting; but if the firing is continued on
"the part of Denmark, Lord Nelson will be obliged to
"set on fire all the floating batteries he has taken,
"without having the power of saving the brave Danes
"who defended them.
"Dated on board His Britannic Majesty's ship
"'Elephant,' Copenhagen Roads, April 2nd, 1801."

The Crown Prince yielding to this demand, and sending
his Adjutant-General to ask an explanation, in reply
Nelson wrote the following note :—

"Lord Nelson's object in sending on shore a flag of

"truce is humanity. He therefore consents that
"hostilities shall cease till Lord Nelson can take his
"prisoners out of the prizes, and he consents to land
"all the wounded Danes and to burn or remove his
"prizes. Lord Nelson, with humble duty to His Royal
"Highness, begs leave to say that he will ever esteem
"it the greatest victory he ever gained, if this flag of
"truce may be the forerunner of a lasting and happy
"union between His Most Gracious Sovereign and
"His Majesty the King of Denmark.

"NELSON AND BRONTE."

The murder of the Russian Emperor, Paul, happening at
this time, influenced decisively the deliberations of the
Danish Government, and a truce of 14 weeks was
therefore signed, Nelson's clear and direct diplomacy
contributing greatly thereto.

He writes to the Right Hon. Henry Addington :—

"My dear Sir, a negotiator is certainly out of my
"line, but being thrown into it I have endeavoured to
"acquit myself as well as I was able, and in such a
"manner as I hope will not entirely merit your
"disapprobation."

After detailing the conditions, and his reasons for
imposing them, he adds a postscript :—

"I have the pleasure to tell you Count Bernstoff was
"too ill to make me a visit yesterday. I had sent him
"a message to leave off his ministerial duplicity, and
"to recollect he had now British admirals to deal with,
"who came with their hearts in their hands. I hate
"the fellow. Colonel Stewart, a very fine gallant man,
"will give you every information."

The anxiety inseparable from the carrying out of these
negotiations, and the annoyance caused by the dilatory
nature and want of decision of Sir Hyde Parker, had made

Nelson receiving the Sword of the wounded Spanish Commodore.

Nelson extremely ill, and he had actually written to Lord St. Vincent, informing him he was unfit to remain where he was, when the Admiralty Order came out for Sir Hyde Parker to return home, and for Nelson to supersede him.

Nelson thereon proceeded to active measures at once and sailed for the Russian coast, as he had before been most anxious to do; but it was too late, and the Russian fleet had escaped into Cronstadt.

His desire had been to make a demonstration which could result in Russia remaining a friend or a foe, as she might elect—taking care his own squadron was in due safety all the time. On receiving a rather discourteous letter from Count Pahlen, he returned a dignified reply, observing :—

> "I have only to regret that my desire to pay a "marked attention to His Imperial Majesty has been "so entirely misunderstood."

This drew forth a humble apology, and the vessel which brought it saluted in leaving.

The contravention of the Armistice by the Danes, countenanced by the Prince Royal himself, made Nelson's position doubly anxious and responsible, but, as usual, his firmness conquered, and the result was a treaty with Russia, which practically put an end to the combination against England, formed by the Northern Powers.

There is a part of Colonel Stewart's narrative too valuable as an example to be omitted. He writes :—

> "The keeping of his fleet continually on the alert, "and thus amply furnishing it with fresh provisions, "were the objects of his lordship's unremitting care ; "and to this may, in a great measure, be ascribed the "uniform good health and discipline which prevailed. "Another point to which he gave nearly equal atten- "tion, was his economy of the resources of the fleet "in regard to stores ; their consumption was as

D

"remarkable for their smallness in the Baltic as it was
"in the fleet afterwards under his command in the
"Mediterranean. His hour of rising was four or five
"o'clock, and of going to rest about ten, breakfast was
"never later than six, and generally nearer five
"o'clock. A midshipman or two were always of the
"party; and I have known him send during the middle
"watch to invite the little fellows to breakfast with
"him when relieved. At table with them he would
"enter into all their boyish tricks, and be the most
"youthful of the party. At dinner he invariably had
"every officer of his ship in turn. The whole ordinary
"business of the fleet was invariably despatched, as it
"had been by Lord St. Vincent, before eight o'clock.

 "The great command of time which Nelson thus
"gave himself, and the alertness which this example
"imparted throughout the whole fleet, can only be
"understood by those who witnessed it, or knew the
"value of early hours."

As soon as possible after hostilities had ceased in the
Baltic Nelson applied to go home, and on leaving issued
the following farewell to the fleet : —

"Lord Nelson has been obliged, from the late very
"bad state of his health, to apply to the Lords Com-
"missioners of the Admiralty for leave to return to
"England, which their Lordships have been pleased to
"comply with. But Lord Nelson cannot allow himself
"to leave the fleet without expressing to the admirals,
"captains, officers, and men, how sensibly he has felt,
"and does feel, all their kindness to him, and also how
"nobly and honourably they have supported him in
"the hour of battle, and the readiness which they have
"shown to maintain the honour of their King and
"country on many occasions which have offered; and
"had more opportunities presented themselves, Lord

" Nelson is firmly persuaded they would have added
" more to the glory of their country.

" Lord Nelson cannot but observe, with the highest
" satisfaction which can fill the breast of a British
" Admiral, that (with the exception of the conduct of
" the officers of two gunbrigs and a bomb), out of eigh-
" teen thousand of which the fleet is composed, not a
" complaint has been made of any officer or man in it ;
" and he cannot but remark that the extraordinary
" health of the fleet, under the blessing of Almighty
" God, is to be attributed to the great regularity, exact
" discipline, and cheerful obedience of every individual
" of the fleet.   The Vice-Admiral assures them that he
" will not fail to represent to the Lords Commissioners
" of the Admiralty their highly praiseworthy conduct ;
" and if it pleases God that the Vice-Admiral should
" recover his health he will feel proud on some future
" day, to go with them in pursuit of further glory, and
" to assist in making the name of our King and country
" beloved and respected by the world.   St. George,
" Kioge Bay, June 18th, 1801."

Ill as he was when he returned to England he allowed
himself but scant rest, for, arriving about the middle of
July, he, without hesitation or delay, took the command of
the English squadron, and on July 27th hoisted his flag on
board the " Unité " at Sheerness, prepared to oppose the
threatened invasion of Buonaparte.

He immediately addressed a most masterly paper to the
Admiralty giving his plans and proposals, and it shows
conclusively how thoroughly he had, even in so short a
time, seized the salient points of the whole situation.

In his first brush with the French he attacked their fleet
off the harbour of Boulogne, sunk five of their ships, and
did them further damage, but the action was little more
than a skirmish, though, as he wrote, it may have shown
the enemy that they "could not with impunity come
outside their ports."   D 2

A second attempt to bring "off the enemy's flotilla, moored in front of Boulogne" failed through "the darkness of the night, with the tide at half-tide," separating the divisions, and preventing all the ships arriving at the same time. He wrote to Lord St. Vincent:—

"I am sorry to tell you that I have not succeeded in "bringing out or destroying the enemy's flotilla "moored in the mouth of the harbour of Boulogne. "The most astonishing bravery was evinced by many "of our officers and men . . . . . upwards of one "hundred killed and wounded. Dear little Parker, his "thigh very much shattered, I have fears for his life. "Langford shot through the leg. The loss has been "heavy, and the object was great. The flotilla, brigs "and flats, were moored by the bottom to the shore "and to each other with chains; therefore, although "several of them were carried, yet the heavy fire of "musketry from the shore, which overlooked them, "forced our people to leave them, without being able, "as I am told, to set them on fire. No person can be "blamed for sending them to the attack but myself; "I knew the difficulty of the undertaking, therefore I "ventured to ask your opinion. . . . . . I own "I shall never bring myself again to allow any attack "to go forward where I am not personally concerned; "my mind suffers much more than if I had a leg shot "off in this late business. Had our force arrived, as I "intended, 'twas not all the chains in France that could "have prevented our folks from bringing off the whole "of the vessels."

Two days later he says:—

"Heavy sea, sick to death—this sea-sickness I shall "never get over."

To Nelson's despatch Lord St. Vincent returned an encouraging and most complimentary letter, but it failed to

lessen Nelson's regret at the failure and for the loss of
officers and men, or to alleviate his suffering anxiety for
Captain Parker, about whom he writes to Dr. Baird : —

"My dear Doctor, your kind letter has given me
"hopes of my dear Parker : he is my child, for I found
"him in distress. I am prepared for the worst,
"although I still hope. Pray tell me as often as you
"can. Would I could be useful, I would come on
"shore and nurse him. I rely on your abilities, and if
"his life is to be spared, that you, under the blessing
"of God, are fully equal to be the instrument. Say
"everything which is kind to Mrs. Parker, and if my
"Parker remembers me, say 'God bless him,' and do
"you believe me your much obliged and thankful
"friend,
                "NELSON AND BRONTE."

Captain Parker succumbed to his wounds, and Nelson
wrote to Dr. Baird : —

"God's will be done. I beg that his hair may be cut
"off and given to me ; it shall remain and be buried
"with me."

From this date (September, 1801) until the end of
October he was "on the watch" in the Channel, but
decisive action was impossible, and that he felt his time
was being wasted this letter to Lord St. Vincent will show :
after writing on service matters he says : —

"I have experienced in the Sound the misery of
"leaving the honour of our country intrusted to pilots,
"who have no other thought than to keep the ship
"clear of danger and their own silly heads clear of
"shot.
"At eight in the morning of 2nd April, not one
"pilot would take charge of a ship. Brierly, who was
"Davidge Gould's master in the 'Audacious,' placed

"boats for me, and fixed my order. Everybody
"knows what I must have suffered; and if any merit
"attaches itself to me, it was in combating the dangers
"of the shallows in défiance of the pilots.

"This boat business must be over; it may be a part
"of a great plan of invasion, but can never be the only
"one; therefore, as our ships cannot act any more in
"lying off the French coast, I own I do not think it is
"now a command for a Vice-Admiral.

"It is not that I want to get a more lucrative
"Mediterranean were vacant to-morrow, that I am
"situation—far from it; I do not know, if the
"equal to undertake it."

Nelson remained in England until May, 1803, when he
left in the "Victory" for the Mediterranean, and commenced the blockade of Toulon, war having been declared
between England and France.

On the 9th July he reports to Mr. Addington:—

"With the casual absence of one or two ships, we
"shall always be seven sail of the line; and as the
"French have at least seven—I believe nine—nearly
"ready, we are in hopes that Buonaparte may be
"angry and order them out, which I have no doubt will
"put our ships in high feather; for I never knew any
"wants after a victory, although we are always full of
"them before."

On the same date he writes to Mr. Davison: —

"The French in Toulon are equal to me at this
"moment, but I do not think they will come out till
"they have a greater superiority. If they do I shall be
"agreeably disappointed. The event, I trust, although
"we are miserably short of men, would be glorious and
"hasten a peace."

For months he remained in the Mediterranean, the
French never giving him an opportunity to fight them, and

he, while cruising about, being continually made anxious by difficulties with deserters, various aggravations from want of stores, from delays, and also from private vexations relating to his estate of Bronte, from which he could never succeed in obtaining any just or certain income, and about which he writes to Mr. Davison (his solicitor) : —

"I shall be truly thankful if you will have the "goodness to put my Bronte estate in a train, that if I "cannot receive the value of it and have done with it, "that at least I may receive the full rental regularly, "for I never will lay out another sixpence on it. ". . . . I told Graefer on first setting out that I "would give up two years' rent for fitting up a house "and improving. I paid more attention to another "sovereign than my own; therefore the King of "Naples' gift of Bronte to me, if it is not now settled "to my advantage, and to be permanent, has cost me a "fortune, and a great deal of favour which I might "have enjoyed, and (much) jealousy which I should "have avoided. I repine not on those accounts. I did "my duty to the Sicilifying my own conscience, and I "am easy. It will be necessary before you take any "steps beyond inquiry, to know from Sir John Acton "what has been done, and what is intended. All that "I beg is that the just thing may be done immediately, "and that I may have it permanent."

On the 27th September he writes to Lord St. Vincent : —

"It is now three months since my last letters were "dated from England, and but for a French news- "paper, which hitherto we have procured through "Spain from Paris, we should not have known how the "world went on; and reports have so often changed "the First Lord of the Admiralty that I know not if I "am now writing to him, but that does not matter; I "trust I am writing to an old friend who sincerely "wishes me as well as I wish him."

On the same date to Mr. Davison : —

> " We are healthy beyond example, and in great good
> " humour with ourselves, and so sharp-set that I
> " would not be a French admiral in the way of any of
> " our ships for something. I believe we are in the
> " right fighting trim, let them come as soon as they
> " please. I never saw a fleet altogether so well
> " officered and manned. Would to God the ships were
> " half as good, but they are what we call crazy."

Orders were given on October the 4th for the blockade
of Genoa, and the home government approved the line of
conduct which Lord Nelson had suggested the Court of
Naples should pursue under the critical circumstances.

His letters and despatches at this time show how entirely
he had continued to keep himself in touch with, and
acquainted with, the designs, politics, and probable intentions of each and every country which was either wholly, or
partially, involved in this war.

He wrote 7th December, 1803, to the Duke of
Clarence : —

> " The French Fleet keep us waiting for them during
> " a long and severe winter's cruise, and such a place as
> " all the Gulf of Lion, for gales of wind from the N.W.
> " to N.E., I never saw, but by always going away large,
> " we generally lose much of their force and the heavy
> " sea of the Gulf. However, by the great care and
> " attention of every captain, we have suffered much
> " less than could have been expected."

He tells Mr. Davison under date December 12th : —

> " My crazy fleet are getting in a very indifferent
> " state, and others will soon follow.
> " The finest ships in the service will soon be
> " destroyed. I know well enough that if I was to go
> " into Malta I should save the ships during this bad

" season. But if I am to watch the French I must be
" at sea, and if at sea must have bad weather and if
" the ships are not fit to stand bad weather, they are
" useless.

" I do not say much, but I do not believe that Lord
" St. Vincent would have kept the sea with such ships.
" But my time of service is nearly over.

" A natural anxiety, of course, must attend my
" station, but, my dear friend, my eyesight fails me
" most dreadfully. I firmly believe that in a very few
" years I shall be stone-blind. It is this only, of all my
" maladies, that makes me unhappy ; but God's will be
" done."

Here may be quoted the invaluable lines Nelson wrote
to a young midshipman : —

" As you from this day start in the world as a man,
" I trust that your future conduct in life will prove you
" both an officer and a gentleman. Recollect that you
" must be a seaman to be an officer, and also that you
" cannot be a good officer without being a gentleman."

For various reasons Nelson never professionally had a
favourable opinion of Malta as an advantageous port or
possession for England, as the following letter to Lord
Hobart clearly illustrates : —

" If we could possess Sardinia we should want
" neither Malta nor any other. This, which is the
" finest island in the Mediterranean, possesses harbours
" fit for arsenals and of a capacity to hold our navy,
" within 24 hours' sail of Toulon ; bays to ride our
" fleets in and to watch both Italy and Toulon. No
" fleet could pass to the eastward between Sicily and
" the Coast of Barbary, nor through the Faro of
" Messina. Malta in point of position is not to be
" named the same year with Sardinia. I
" venture to predict that if we do not, the French will
" get possession of that island. . . . The country

"is fruitful beyond idea, and abounds in cattle and
"sheep, and would in corn, wine, and oil. It has no
"manufactories. . . . . It is worth any money to
"obtain, and I pledge my existence it could be held for
"as little as Malta in its establishment, and produce a
"larger revenue."

There is a letter to Mr. Elliot about this time saying:—

"We have had a most terrible winter: it has almost
"knocked me up. I have been very ill, and am now
"far from recovered, but I hope to hold out till the
"battle is over, when I must recruit myself for further
"exertion."

His ships had been reduced from seven to six sail-of-the-
line, and all were under considerable "want of cordage,
sails, and other stores," which had been sent out from
England in quite inadequate quantities. There was a
question of the English fleet going to Gibraltar, when the
mail between Antibes and Corsica was captured, and
Nelson sent the following order to Captain Parker:—

"An invasion of Sardinia is intended immediately
"on our departure, by the French from Corsica. It is,
"therefore, my direction that you remain at your
"present anchorage, and use your utmost endeavours
"in preventing the invasion of the French, and give
"every aid and assistance in your power to the inhabi-
"tants, should it be attempted."

He also wrote to Lord Hobart, 6th January, 1804:—

"However (great) my distress is, and greater it
"cannot well be, for frigates and sloops, yet I could
"not allow the most important island and naval station
"in the Mediterranean to fall, whilst I have any means
"of preventing it."

The spring found Nelson still looking out for the French,

hoping, as he expressed it, that "we shall some day get at them." The French Admiral La Touche Tréville (the same who had been opposed to Nelson at Boulogne) was continually coming out of Toulon, and going in again without giving battle, and at last he actually accused Nelson of having run away from him! He wrote a gasconading letter on the subject, which was discovered at Malta and forwarded to Nelson, who remarks in a letter to the Rev. W. Nelson : —

"I have been expecting Monsieur La Touche to give "me the meeting every day for this year past, and "only hope he will come out before I go hence. ". . . . . You will have seen his letter of how he "chased me and how I ran. I keep it ; and, by God, "if I take him he shall eat it."

On August 9th he writes to Mr. Davison : —

"I am expecting Monsieur La Touche (as he has "wrote a letter that I ran away) to come out of his "nest. The whole history was too contemptible for "my notice, but I have thought it right, not upon my "own account, but for the satisfaction of the "Admiralty, etc., etc., to send a copy of the 'Victory's' "log ; for, if my character for *not* running away is not "fixed by this time, it is not worth my trouble to put "the world right at my time of life.''

In the same month he was suffering greatly, and wrote to the home authorities that "with much uneasiness of mind" he felt it his duty to report that the state of his health made it absolutely necessary he should return to England to re-establish it ; and he continues : —

"No officer could be placed in a more enviable "command than the one I have the honour to be "placed in, and no command ever produced so much "happiness to a commander-in-Chief, whether in the

"flag-officers, the captains, or the good conduct of the
"crews of every ship in this fleet, and the constant
"marks of approbation for my conduct which I have
"received from every Court in the Mediterranean leave
"me nothing to wish for but a better state of health."
On the 4th October he writes to Sir A. J. Ball:—

"I think I see much too close a connection between
"France and Austria, and we know the Turks would
"jump to join such an alliance. . . . I wish my
"health were better. . . Toulon was safe on
"Sunday last, as Boyle will tell you. No admiral has
"hoisted his flag in the room of La Touche; he is
"gone, and all his lies with him. The French papers
"say he died in consequence of walking so often up to
"the signal post upon Sepet to watch us; I always
"pronounced that that would be his death."

Vice-Admiral La Touche Tréville died on the 18th
August, and Buonaparte appointed Vice-Admiral Villeneuve to succeed him, with orders that he should leave
Toulon if possible before the 21st October, taking with him
6,000 or 7,000 troops. The French fleet (believed then to
consist of 11 ships-of-the-line and 7 or 8 frigates) was to
sail out of the Mediterranean, retake Goree, ravage the
British Settlements on the African Coast, and capture the
island of St. Helena. Thence to steer to Cayenne,
eventually take the island of Dominique, place under
contribution all the British West India Islands, capture or
burn the vessels lying there, and leave certain of their ships
in the Antilles in order to hamper English trading. The
first attempt to leave Toulon failed, and Mons. Jurien de la
Gravière writes:—

"A first essay was destined to establish the immense
"difference which cannot but exist between a fleet
"inured to labour, and another just escaped from the
"idleness of a port. On January 19th, 1805, Nelson
"was at anchor in Agincourt Roads, where two of his

" frigates, the 'Active' and 'Seahorse,' appeared at
" the entrance of the Straits of Bonifacio under a press
" of sail with the long expected signal, ' the enemy is
" at sea.'

"It was three o'clock in the afternoon when they
" anchored near the 'Victory,' and at half past four the
" English Fleet was under sail. It becomes dark there
" about five o'clock at that time of the year ; the wind
" was blowing strong from the westward, and the fleet
" could not work to windward against it. So that it
" was necessary to go through one of the Eastern
" passages which open into the Tuscan Sea. Though
" it was now completely dark, Nelson took the lead in
" the 'Victory,' and resolved to conduct his eleven
" ships-of-the-line between the rocks of Biscia
" and the North-east extremity of Sardinia. This
" passage, whose breadth does not exceed a quarter of
" a mile, has never since been attempted by any fleet.
" The English squadron cleared it, formed in a single
" line ahead, each ship showing a light astern to guide
" the one which followed."

On the successful issue of this masterly endeavour,
Nelson despatched a frigate on the look out for the French
fleet. The next day two other frigates left. A heavy gale
continued for two days, and the frigates returned with no
news of the enemy. On the 19th the " Phœbe" joined,
reporting that the French ship "Indomptable" was lying
disabled on the West coast of Corsica.

Nelson sent again in all directions to find the enemy, but
failed, and being persuaded the French were gone to
Egypt, he steered to the eastward.

At Alexandria there was no news, and Nelson left again
for Malta, and not until some days after did he hear from
Naples that the fleet of Mons. Villeneuve had encountered
a severe gale in the Gulf of Lyons, and with the exception
of four damaged vessels had put back again into Toulon.

It was while sailing back from Malta to Sardinia that
Nelson wrote his noble letter to Lord Melville, then First
Lord of the Admiralty.   He writes on the 14th February
(1805) :—

> " Feeling, as I do, that I am entirely responsible to
> " my King and country for the whole of my conduct, I
> " find no difficulty at this moment, when I am so
> " unhappy at not finding the French fleet, nor having
> " obtained the smallest information where they are, to
> " lay before you the whole of the reasons which
> " induced me to pursue the line of conduct I have done.
> " I have consulted no man, therefore the whole blame
> " of ignorance in forming my judgment must rest with
> " me.   I would allow no man to take from me an atom
> " of glory had I fallen in with the French fleet, nor do
> " I desire any man to partake of any of the responsi-
> " bility.   All is mine, right or wrong : therefore I shall
> " now state my reasons, after seeing that Sardinia,
> " Naples, and Sicily were safe, for believing that
> " Egypt was the destination of the French fleet ; and
> " at this moment of sorrow I still feel that I have acted
> " right.   Firstly, the wind had blown from north-east
> " to south-west for 14 days before they sailed ; there-
> " fore they might without difficulty have gone to the
> " westward.   Secondly, they came out with gentle
> " breezes at north-west, and north-north-west.   Had
> " they been bound to Naples, the most natural thing
> " for them to have done would have been to run along
> " their own shore to the eastward, where they would
> " have ports every 20 leagues of coast to take shelter in.
> " Thirdly, they bore away in the evening of the 18th,
> " with a strong gale at north-west or north-north-west
> " steering south, or south-by-west.   It blew so hard
> " that the ' Seahorse ' went more than 13 knots an
> " hour to get out of their way.   Desirable as Sardinia
> " is for them, they could get it without risking their

" fleet, although certainly not so quickly as by
" attacking Cagliari. However, I left nothing to
" chance in that respect, and therefore went off to
" Cagliari. Having afterwards gone to Sicily, both to
" Palermo and Messina, and thereby given encourage-
" ment for a defence, and knowing all was safe at
" Naples, I had only the Morea and Egypt to look to.
" For although I knew one of the French ships was
" crippled, yet I considered the character of Buona-
" parte ; and that the orders given by him on the banks
" of the Seine would not take into consideration wind
" or weather. Nor, indeed, could the accident of even
" three or four ships alter, in my opinion, a destination
" of importance : therefore such an accident did not
" weigh in my mind, and I went first to Morea, and
" then to Egypt. The result of my enquiries at Coron
" and Alexandria confirms me in my former opinion ;
" and therefore, my lord, if my obstinacy or ignorance
" is so gross, I should be the first to recommend your
" superseding me. But, on the contrary, if, as I flatter
" myself, it should be found that my ideas of the
" probable destination of the French fleet were well
" founded, in the opinion of His Majesty's ministers,
" then I shall hope for the consolation of having my
" conduct approved by His Majesty ; who will, I am
" sure, weigh my whole proceedings in the scale of
" justice."

Baffled continually by contrary winds and by a run of
what can only be characterized as " ill luck," Nelson cruised
on until April (1805). On the 13th March he had written
to the Admiralty : —

> " Their Lordships are fully aware of my reasons for
> " not attending to my own health since I received
> " their permission to return to England for its re-
> " establishment.
> " I do assure you that no consideration for self could

H.M.S. Victory sailing into action at the Battle of Trafalgar.

after them, his force consisting of eleven ships only, theirs of eighteen.

Unhappily, through the intelligence given him by General Brereton being incorrect, he missed the French at St. Lucia, followed them with continued ill-success to Tobago, Trinidad, Grenada, and Antigua, whence he again sailed in pursuit, not despairing of " getting up with them before they arrive at Cadiz or Toulon," to which ports he thought they were bound. In his own mind he had credited the French with other intentions, though forced to act according to the information given him, and he writes : —

> " My opinion is as firm as a rock, that some cause,
> " orders, or inability to perform any service in these
> " seas, has made them resolve to proceed direct for
> " Europe, sending the Spanish ships to the Havana.
> " There would have been no occasion for opinions,
> " had not General Brereton sent his damned intelli-
> " gence from St. Lucia ; nor would I have received it
> " to have acted by it, but I was assured that his
> " information was very correct. It has almost broke
> " my heart, but I must not despair."

On June 12th he writes to the Duke of Clarence —

> " Your Royal Highness will easily conceive the
> " misery I am feeling at hitherto having missed the
> " French fleet, and entirely owing to false information
> " sent from St. Lucia, which arrived at Barbadoes the
> " evening of July 3rd. . . . But for that informa-
> " tion, I should have been off Port Royal as they were
> " putting to sea, and our battle would have been fought
> " where the brave Rodney beat De Grasse."

To Mr. Davison he says : —

> " I resisted the opinion of General Brereton's
> information till it would have been the height of
> presumption to have carried my disbelief further. I

E

"could not in the face of General and Admiral go
"N.W. when it was *apparently* clear that the enemy
"had gone S.—But I am miserable. . . . I can
"say nothing, or think anything, but the loss my
"country has sustained by General Brereton's unfor-
"tunate, ill-timed, false information."

He notes in his diary on the 18th July:—

"Cape Spartel in sight, but no French fleet, nor any
"information about them; how sorrowful this makes
"me, but I cannot help myself!"

To Mr. W. Marsden on the 20th July, Tetuan Bay:—

"I have to acquaint you that I anchored in this Bay
"yesterday without having obtained the smallest
"intelligence of the enemy's fleet, except what is
"contained in the inclosed paper" (alluding to a
boarding report of "The Sally").

In his diary on the same day he writes:—

"I went on shore for the first time since 16th June,
"1803; and from having my foot out of the 'Victory'
"two years, wanting ten days."

Professor Laughton records:—

"On the 24th July, the 'Decade' frigate joined from
"Admiral Collingwood, yet still no information of the
"enemy. On the 25th the 'Termagant' joined, with
"an account that the combined fleet had been seen by
"the 'Curieux' brig on 19th June, standing to the
"northward."

Sir Robert Calder, however, had the good fortune to
meet the French fleet towards the end of July, and to gain
the victory. On August 16th, Nelson writes to Captain
Fremantle:—

"I could not last night sit down to thank you for

"your truly kind letter, and for your large packet of
"newspapers, for I was in truth bewildered by the
"account of Sir Robert Calder's victory, and the joy
"of the event, together with the hearing that John
"Bull was not content, which I am sorry for. Who
"can, my dear Freemantle, command all the success
"which our country may wish? We have fought
"together, and therefore well know what it is. I have
"had the best disposed fleet of friends, but who can
"say what will be the event of a battle? And it most
"sincerely grieves me, that in any of the papers it
"should be insinuated that Lord Nelson could have
"done better. I should have fought the enemy, so did
"my friend Calder; but who can say that he will be
"more successful than another? I only wish to stand
"on my own merits, and not by comparison, one way
"or the other, upon the conduct of a brother officer."

On the 18th August he reports having joined Admiral
Cornwallis off Ushant, and, having received orders from
that admiral to do so, had proceeded immediately with the
"Victory" and "Superb" to Spithead, where he had
arrived that morning.

The next day Lord Nelson went to his own house at
Merton.

There is a letter from Lord Minto, saying:—

"I met Lord Nelson, in August, 1805, in a mob in
"Piccadilly. I got hold of his arm, so that I was
"mobbed too. It is really quite affecting to see the
"wonder and admiration and love and respect of the
"whole world; and the genuine expression of all these
"sentiments at once, from gentle and simple, the
"moment he is seen. It is beyond anything repre-
"sented in a play or a poem of fame."

While at Merton he refused all invitations to stay away,
as all his own family were coming to visit him, but on the

1st September Captain Honble. H. Blackwood (H.M.S. Euryalus) brought the news of the arrival at Cadiz of the combined fleets. Captain Blackwood, on his way to London, called on Nelson at 5 a.m., found him up and dressed, and immediately on hearing the news Nelson followed him to town.

It was at once decided Nelson should go out to Cadiz in the "Victory" in command of the British fleet.

It is related by Mr. Lathom Browne, that—

"At the Admiralty the First Lord told him to "choose the officers he would like to have under his "command. 'Choose them yourself,' replied Nelson, "'the same spirit animates the whole navy: you "cannot go wrong.' Wisely he was given unlimited "powers, and his secretary desired to give the names "of the ships which he wished to be added to his "command."

In a letter, dated 6th September, to Mr. Davison he says :—

"I hope my absence will not be long, and that I "shall soon meet the combined fleets with a force "sufficient to do the job well; for half a victory would "but half content me. But I do not believe the "Admiralty can give me a force within fifteen or "sixteen sail-of-the-line of the enemy; and, therefore, "if every ship took her opponent, we should have to "contend with a fresh fifteen or sixteen sail-of-the-line. "But I will do my best, and I hope God Almighty will "go with me. I have much to lose and little to gain; "and I go because it is right, and will serve my country "faithfully."

On the same day he also wrote :—

"I send you a memorandum which I am sure you "will comply with. Poor blind Mrs. Nelson I must

"assist this morning. A Mr. Brand, an apothecary,
"called upon me for £133 2s. 6d., as due from my
"brother Maurice to him. I shall refer him to you,
"and if it is a just demand, he must have it."

This Mrs. Nelson was the widow of his brother Maurice.
On Friday, the 13th of September, 1805, he started, and
this entry is found in his private diary:—

"At half-past ten drove from dear, dear Merton,
"where I left all which I hold dear in this world, to go
"to serve my King and my country. May the great
"God whom I adore enable me to fulfil the expecta-
"tions of my country; and if it is His good pleasure
"that I should return, my thanks will never cease
"being offered up to the throne of His mercy. If it
"is His good Providence to cut short my days upon
"earth, I bow with the greatest submission, relying
"that he will protect those dear to me that I may leave
"behind. His will be done. Amen, Amen, Amen."

On the 14th he embarked on board the "Victory" at
Portsmouth, sailed on the 15th, and wrote off Portland on
the 16th to Mr. Davison:—

"I am gone and beating down Channel with a foul
"wind. . . . Poor blind Mrs. Nelson, I have given
"£150 to pay her debts, and I intend to pay her house
"rent in future, in addition to the £200 a year, which
"I take it will be about £40 a year."

Passing Gibraltar about September 30th, he writes on
that date:—

"My dear Ball, I got fairly into the fleet yesterday,
"and under all circumstances I find them as perfect as
"could be expected. . . . The force is at present
"not so large as might be wished, but I will do my
"best with it; they will give me more when they can,
"and I am not come forth to find difficulties, but to
"remove them."

October the 9th is the date on which Nelson issued to his fleet his celebrated plan of attack—surnamed the "Nelson touch," and it is to be regretted that its length precludes the insertion of it here.   When he explained it to the officers of the fleet—

> " All approved it was new—it was singular—it was
> " simple ; and from the admiral downwards it was
> " repeated, 'it must succeed, if they will allow us to get
> " at them!' "

On that day (October 9th) he wrote to Admiral Collingwood : —

> " I send you my plan of attack, as far as a man dare
> " venture to guess at the very uncertain position the
> " enemy may be found in.   But, my dear friend, it is to
> " place you perfectly at ease respecting my intentions
> " and to give full scope to your judgment for carrying
> " them into effect.   We can, my dear Coll, have no
> " little jealousies.   We have only one great object in
> " view, that of annihilating our enemies, and getting a
> " glorious peace for our country.   No man has more
> " confidence in another than I have in you ; and no
> " man will render your services more justice than your
> " very old friend,
>
> " NELSON AND BRONTE."

He wrote in his diary the same day : —

> " Fresh breezes easterly.   Received an account from
> " Blackwood, that the French ships had all bent their
> " top-gallant sails.   Sent the 'Pickle' to him, with
> " orders to keep a good look-out.   Sent Admiral
> " Collingwood the Nelson touch.   At night wind
> " westerly."

To Captain Blackwood he writes on the 10th : —

> " I rely on you that we can't miss getting hold of
> " them, and I will give them such a shaking as they

"never yet experienced; at least I will lay down my
"life in the attempt. We are a very powerful fleet
"and not to be held cheap."

On October 13th he reports to the Admiralty : —

"His Majesty's ships 'Agamemnon' and 'L'Aim-
"able' joined this forenoon, and the 'Prince of Wales,'
"bearing the flag of Vice-Admiral Sir Robert Calder,
"leaves the fleet this evening with orders to proceed
"direct to Spithead. The Vice-Admiral takes with
"him the captains of His Majesty's ships 'Thunderer'
"and 'Ajax,' whom I have permitted to accompany
"him, for the purpose of attending the Court requested
"by that officer on his late conduct between the 22nd
"and 25th of July last, which I hope, for the reasons I
"have before stated, their Lordships will be pleased to
"approve of."

It will be remembered how Sir Robert Calder had
allowed his jealousy of Nelson to find expression after the
battle of St. Vincent, and yet we here find Nelson affording
him every facility to clear his character, even to the sending
home of officers, and of a ship, which could be but ill spared
at that critical moment. We read also in a lettter to
Captain Hamond : —

"Sir Robert Calder has just left us to stand his trial,
"which I think of a very serious nature. God send
"him a good deliverance."

Tn his private diary he writes on October 19th : —

"Fine weather, wind easterly. At half-past nine
"the 'Mars,' being one of the look-out ships, repeated
"the signal 'that the enemy was coming out of port.'
"Made the signal for a 'general chase S.E.'; wind at
"south, Cadiz bearing E.N.E. by compass, distant
"sixteen leagues. At three the 'Colossus' made the
"signal 'that the enemy's fleet was at sea.' In the

' evening directed the fleet to observe my motions
' during the night, and for ' Britannia,' ' Prince,' and
' Dreadnought,' they being heavy sailers, to take their
' stations as convenient; and for ' Mars,' ' Orion,'
' " Belleisle,' ' Leviathan,' ' Bellerophon,' and Poly-
' phemus,' to go ahead during the night, and to carry a
' light, standing for the Strait's mouth."

On October the 20th, he notes : —

" Fresh breezes S.S.W. and rainy. Communicated
" with ' Phœbe,' ' Defence,' and ' Colossus,' who saw
" near forty sail of ships of war outside of Cadiz
" yesterday evening ; but the wind being southerly
" they could not get to the mouth of the Straits. We
" were between Trafalgar and Cape Spartel. The
" frigates made the signal that they saw nine sail
" outside the harbour ; gave the frigates instructions
" for their guidance, and placed ' Defence,' ' Colossus,'
" and ' Mars ' between me and the frigates. At noon
' fresh gales and heavy rain ; Cadiz N.E. 9 leagues.
" In the afternoon Captain Blackwood telegraphed
" that the enemy seemed determined to go to the west-
' ward ; and that they shall *not* do, if in the power of
' Nelson and Bronte to prevent them.
" At 5 telegraphed Captain Blackwood that I relied
" upon his keeping sight of the enemy. At 6 o'clock
" ' Naiad ' made the signal of 31 sail of the enemy
" N.N.E. The frigates and the look-out ships kept
" sight of the enemy most admirably all night, and
" told me by signals which tack they were upon. At
" 8 we wore, and stood to S.W., and at 4 a.m. wore,
" stood to the N.E."

On the 21st of October, 1805, is the last entry of all in
his diary : —

· [" At daylight saw the enemy's combined fleet from
" East to E.S.E. ; bore away ; made the signal for

" order of sailing, and to prepare for battle ; the enemy
" with their heads to the southward : at seven the
" the enemy wearing in succession. May the Great
" God, whom I worship, grant to my country, and for
" the benefit of Europe in general, a great and glorious
" victory ; and may no misconduct in any one tarnish
" it ; and may humanity after victory be the
" predominant feature in the British fleet. For myself,
" individually, I commit my life to Him who made me,
" and may His blessing light upon my endeavours for
" serving my country faithfully. To Him I resign
" myself and the just cause which is entrusted to me to
" defend. Amen. Amen. Amen."

These are the last written words of Nelson, and for the
end we must turn to the narratives of others.

The " Orion's " log gives, 21st October :—

" A.M.—At 6.15 answered the general signal 76
" (bear up and sail large) ; saw the enemy's fleet to the
" eastward—33 sail of the line. . . cleared ship for
" action."

The log of the " Téméraire " records :—

" Noon.—Running down for the enemy. P.M.—
" Light winds running down with lower top-mast and
" top-gallant studding-sails set on the larboard side,
" within a ship's length of the ' Victory,' running for
" the 14th ship of the enemy's line from the van. 15
" minutes past noon, cut away the studding-sails and
" hauled to the wind. At 18 minutes past noon, the
" enemy began to fire ; 20 minutes past noon, the
" ' Victory' opened her fire ; immediately put our helm
" a-port to shear clear of the ' Victory ' and opened our
" fire against the ' Santissima Trinidad,' and two ships
" ahead of her, when the action became general. Some
" time after, the ' Victory' falling on board her
" opponent, the ' Téméraire ' being closely engaged on

"both sides, the ship on the larboard side, engaging
"the 'Victory,' fell alongside of us, the 'Victory' on
"her larboard side, the yard arms locked, and
"immediately after struck and was boarded by some
"of the officers and part of the crew of us, at the same
"time being engaged with one of the enemy on the
"starboard side, a Spanish three-deck ship being on
"the larboard bow, or nearly ahead, who had raked us
"during great part of the action.   About 10 or 15
"minutes past 2, the enemy's ship on the starboard
"side fell alongside of us, on which we immediately
"boarded her and struck her colours."

The following is selected from the graphic and nobly
impartial account of the battle by Captain Jurien de la
Gravière : —

"Divided at first into two lines, of which Colling-
"wood led the one in the 'Royal Sovereign,' and
"Nelson the other in the 'Victory,' the British fleet
"steadily neared their enemy, who had now, by
"wearing together, turned their heads to Cadiz.
"Eleven sail followed the 'Royal Sovereign,' and
"fifteen the 'Victory.'"

Of the combined fleets eighteen were French ships,
eighty and seventy-four guns, and fifteen Spanish ships, of
which four were three-deckers.   The French and Spanish
ships were intermixed, and though at—

"The commencement of the action the British
"formed only two lines, during its course four ships of
"Collingwood's column separated themselves from
"their companions, and made a dash at the rear ships
"of the combined fleet.
"The fleets were now within a few miles of each
"other, when Nelson, having made all necessary
"signals, asked Captain Blackwood, of the 'Euryalus,'
"whether he did not think one more was wanting.

" Reflecting for a few minutes he called the acting
" signal lieutenant (Mr. Pasco) to him. 'Make signal
" to the fleet that England confides that every man will
" do his duty," Pasco suggested 'expects,' as there was
" a signal for that word in the vocabulary. Nelson
" consented,. and added, 'Make it quickly, as I have
" one more signal to make—Close action.' Then at
" 11.15 flew out the flags of that ever-memorable
" signal.

" ' England expects that every man will do his duty.'

" ' Now,' said Nelson, 'I can do no more, we must
" trust to the great Dispenser of all events, and the
" justice of our cause. I thank God for this great
" opportunity of doing my duty.'

" When Blackwood suggested that he should
" transfer his flag to some other ship in a less exposed
" situation, 'No, Blackwood,' replied Nelson, 'on such
" occasions as these it is the Commander-in-Chief's
" duty to set the example.' Feigning to yield to the
" entreaties of others, Nelson allowed the order to be
" given to the ' Téméraire,' 'Neptune,' and 'Leviathan,'
" to take the lead, but very soon after, by making more
" sail on the "Victory,' he rendered the execution of
" the order impossible . . . . . . It was noon.
" The flag of St. George, with the red cross, was flying
" along the English line, while with reiterated cries of
" ' Vive l'Empereur,' the French fleet hoisted the
" tricolour ; the Spaniards at the same time the banner
" of Castile, and suspending a large wooden cross
" beneath it. At this moment Villeneuve gave the
" signal of battle. A single gun, aimed at the ' Royal
" Sovereign,' immediately burst from the ' Fougueux,'
" and was quickly followed by a rolling fire to which
" no English ship replied. The ' Royal Sovereign '
" was then nearly a mile ahead of the ' Belleisle,' and
" about two miles from the ' Victory.' Still, uninjured
" by this ill-directed fire, she bore down on the ' Santa

Anna,' singly, silently, unswervingly, as if protected
by some secret spell. The crew, lying down at their
quarters, presented no object to the few shots which
struck' her hull, and the stray ball which boomed
through her masts had not yet done any injury.

" ' Rotheram,' said Collingwood to his flag-captain,
when, 'after bearing the fire of the combined fleets for
ten minutes, he was about to plunge into the ranks
of our rear-squadron, ' What would not Nelson give
to be 'here now ?' ' See,' said Nelson, at the same
instant, ' how that noble fellow, Collingwood, takes
his ship into action.'

" The ' Fougueux' vainly endeavoured to bar the
way ; 'from the triple tiers of the ' Royal Sovereign '
burst 'a dense storm of shot and smoke. Each gun
doubly charged, poured its contents into the stern of
the ' Santa Anna.' One hundred and fifty cannon
balls swept the decks of that ship, and left four
hundred men stretched upon them. The 'Royal
Sovereign ' then ranged up to leeward, engaged the
Spanish vice-admiral yard-arm to yard-arm ; but she
soon had other enemies to contend with. The ' San
Leandro,' ' San Juste,' and ' Indomptable' closed up
to surround her. 'Fougueux' opened obliquely
upon her, and her sails were soon in shreds. Nevertheless, in the midst of that hailstorm of shot, which
were seen striking each other in the air, the ' Royal
Sovereign ' did not less furiously cannonade the
enemy she had singled out. The Spaniard's fire
slackened, and above the clouds of smoke which
enveloped the heroic group, Nelson's anxious eye
could 'still discover the lofty flag of Collingwood."

The log of the " Victory " records : —

" At noon, standing for the enemy's tenth ship with
all possible sail set. . . Light airs and cloudy.
. . . At four minutes to twelve, opened our fire
on the enemy's van, in keeping down their line. At

"twenty minutes past twelve, in attempting to pass
"through the enemy's line, we fell on board the tenth
"and eleventh ships, when the action became general.
"About 1.15 (Lord Nelson) was wounded in the
"shoulder. At 1.30 the 'Redoubtable' having struck
"her colours, we ceased firing our starboard guns, but
"continued engaged with the 'Santissima Trinidad,'
"and some of the enemy's ships on the larboard side.
"Observed the 'Téméraire' between the 'Redoubt-
"able' and another French ship of the line, both of
"which had struck. The action continued general
"until 3 o'clock, when several of the enemy's ships
"around us had struck. Observed the 'Royal
"Sovereign' with the loss of her main and mizen
"masts, and some of the enemy's ships around her
"dismasted. At 3.10 observed 4 sail of the enemy's
"van tack, and stood along our line to windward, fired
"our larboard guns at those which could reach them.

"At 3.40 made the signal for our ships to keep their
"wind and engage the enemy's van coming along our
"weather line. At 4.15 the Spanish rear-admiral to
"windward struck to some of our ships which had
"tacked after them. Observed one of the enemy's
"ships blow up, and fourteen sail of the enemy's ships
"standing towards Cadiz, and three sail of the enemy's
"ships standing to southward. Partial firing continued
"until 4.30, when a victory being reported to Lord
"Nelson, he then died of his wounds."

In reporting to the Admiralty the—

"Ever-to-be-lamented death of Vice-Admiral Lord
"Viscount Nelson, who, in the late conflict with the
"enemy, fell in the hour of victory,"

Admiral Collingwood proceeds :—

"Such a battle could not be fought without
"sustaining a great loss of men. I have not only to

"lament, in common with the British navy and the
"British nation, in the fall of the Commander-in-Chief,
"the loss of a hero whose name will be immortal, and
"his memory ever dear to his country, but my heart is
"rent with the most poignant grief for the death of a
"friend to whom, by many years of intimacy and a
"perfect knowledge of the virtues of his mind, which
"inspired ideas superior to the common race of men, I
"was bound by the strongest ties of affection ; a grief
"to which even the glorious occasion in which he fell
" does not bring the consolation which perhaps it ought."

All narratives are unanimous in their accounts of the
danger to which Nelson was exposed—and voluntarily
exposed—throughout the commencement of the action.

In " James's Naval History " the account is given of how
often he, with his remaining eye—

"Cast an anxious glance towards the Franco-
"Spanish line in search of the ship which he meant
"the 'Victory' first to grapple with ; and so lightly did
"Lord Nelson value personal risk, that, although urged
"more than once on the subject, he would not suffer
"those barriers from the enemy's grape and musketry,
"the hammocks, to be placed one inch higher than—
"to facilitate his view of objects around him—they
"were accustomed to be stowed. . . . At length
"a shot went through the 'Victory's' maintop-gallant-
"sail, affording to the enemy the first visible proof that
"his shot would reach.
"A minute or two of awful silence ensued ; and
"then, as if by signal from the French Admiral, the
"whole van, or at least seven or eight of the weather-
"most ships, opened a fire upon the 'Victory,' such a
"fire as had scarcely before been directed at a single
"ship. In a few minutes a round shot killed Mr. John
"Scott, Lord Nelson's public secretary, while he was
"conversing with Captain Hardy. . . Just as she

" got within about 500 yards of the larboard-beam of
" the ' Bucentaure,' the ' Victory's ' mizen top-mast was
" shot away about two-thirds up. A shot also struck
" and knocked to pieces the wheel, and the ship was
" obliged to be steered in the gun room. . .

" Presently a shot, that had come through a thick-
" ness of four hammocks near the larboard cross-tree,
" and had carried away part of the larboard quarter of
the launch as she lay on the booms, struck the fore-
" brace bits on the quarter-deck, and passed between
" Lord Nelson and Captain Hardy; a splinter from
the bits bruising the left foot of the latter, and
" tearing the buckle from his shoe. ' They both,' says Dr.
" Beatty, ' instantly stopped, and were observed by the
" officers on deck to survey each other with enquiring
" looks, each supposing the other to be wounded.'

" His Lordship then smiled and said, ' This is too
" warm work, Hardy, to last long,' and declared that
" through all the battles he had been in, he had never
" witnessed more cool courage than was displayed by
" the ' Victory's ' crew on this occasion. In a few
" seconds afterwards, as the ' Bucentaure ' slowly
" forged ahead, a large French ship was seen upon her
" lee-quarter, and another ship astern of the former in
" the act of ranging up, as if with the intention of
" completely closing the interval. Now it was that
" Captain Hardy represented to Lord Nelson the
" impracticability of passing through the line without
" running on board one of the ships. His Lordship
quickly replied, ' I cannot help it ; it does not signify
" which we run on board of—go on board which you
" please ; take your choice.' At this moment . . .
. . . the loss on board the ' Victory ' amounted to
" twenty officers and men killed and thirty wounded ;
" a loss that would have been still more severe had not
" the enemy's guns been pointed at the rigging and the
" sails, rather than at the hull of the ship. In conse-

Death of Lord Nelson in the Cockpit of H.M.S. Victory. October 21st, 1805.

"was of the same destructive character as the broad-
"side poured by the 'Royal Sovereign' into the stern
"of the 'Santa Anna.' The account which the
"'Bucéntaure's' officers gave, as the extent of their
"loss in killed and wounded by the 'Victory's' fire, was
"'nearly 400 men.'

"Never allowing mere personal comfort to interfere
"with what he considered to be the good of the service,
"Lord Nelson, when the 'Victory' was fitting to
"receive his flag, ordered the large skylight over his
"cabin to be removed, and the space planked up, so as
"to afford him a walk amidships clear of the guns and
"ropes. Here, along an extent of deck of about
"twenty-one feet, bound abaft by the stancheon
"wheel, and forward by the combings of the cabin
"ladder way, were the Admiral and Captain Hardy
"during the whole of the operations we have just
"detailed. . . . . At about 1h. 25m. p.m., just as
"the two had arrived within one pace of the regular
"turning spot at the cabin ladder way, Lord Nelson,
"who, regardless of quarter-deck etiquette, was
"walking on the larboard side, suddenly faced about.
"Captain Hardy, as soon as he had taken the other
"step, turned also, and saw the Admiral in the act of
"falling. He was then on his knees with his left hand
"just touching the deck. The arm giving way Lord
"Nelson fell on his left side, exactly upon the spot
"where his secretary, Mr. Scott, had breathed his last,
"and with whose blood his lordship's clothes were
"soiled. On Captain Hardy's expressing a hope that
"he was not severely wounded, Lord Nelson replied,
"'They have done for me at last, Hardy.' 'I hope
"not,' answered Captain Hardy. 'Yes, my backbone
"is shot through.' The wound was by a musket ball,
"which had entered the left shoulder through the fore
"part of the epaulet, and, descending, had lodged in
"the spine.

F

"That the wound had been given by some one
"stationed in the 'Redoubtable's' mizen-top was
"rendered certain, not only from the nearness (about
"fifteen yards), and situation of the mizen top in
"reference to the course of the ball, but from the
"circumstance that the French ship's maintop was
"screened by a portion of the 'Victory's' mainsail as
"it hung when clewed up."

The following extracts are taken from the narrative of
Dr. Beatty, surgeon of the "Victory" :—

"The Captain ordered the seamen to carry the
"Admiral to the cockpit. . . . . While the men
"were carrying him down the ladder from the middle
"deck . . . . he took his handkerchief from his
"pocket and covered his face with it, that he might be
"conveyed to the cockpit at this crisis unnoticed by the
"crew. . . . The surgeon had examined these
"two officers and found them dead, when his attention
"was arrested by several of the wounded calling to him
"'Mr. Beatty, Lord Nelson is here; Mr. Beatty, the
"Admiral is wounded.' The surgeon, on looking
"round, saw the handkerchief fall from his lordship's
"face, when the stars on his coat, which had also been
"covered by it, appeared. Mr. Burke, the purser, and
"the surgeon ran immediately to his lordship's
"assistance, and took him from the arms of the seamen
"who had carried him below.

"In conveying him to one of the midshipmen's
"berths, they stumbled, but recovered themselves
"without falling. Lord Nelson then enquired who was
"supporting him, and when the surgeon informed him,
"his lordship replied: 'Ah, Mr. Beatty! You can do
"nothing for me. I have but a short time to live, my
"back is shot through.' The surgeon said, 'He hoped
"the wound was not so dangerous as his lordship
"imagined, and that he might still survive long to enjoy

" his glorious victory.' The Rev. Dr. Scott . . .
" now came instantly . . . . and in his anguish of
" grief, wrung his hands and said, 'Ah! Beatty, how
" prophetic you were,' alluding to the apprehensions
" expressed by the surgeon for his lordship's safety
" previous to the battle. He was laid upon a bed,
" stripped of his clothes, and covered with a sheet.
" While this was effecting, he said to Dr. Scott, ' Doctor,
" I told you so : I am gone.' His wound was here
" examined, but he was not then told it was a fatal one.

" Then came an ardent thirst. He called frequently
" for drink and to be fanned with paper. ' Fan, fan,
" drink, drink.' This he continued to do until a very
" few minutes before he expired. Mr. Burke told him
" the enemy were decisively defeated, and that he
" hoped that he would still live to be the bearer of the
" joyful news. ' It is nonsense, Mr. Burke, to suppose
" I can live. My sufferings are great, but they will all
" be soon over.' Dr. Scott entreated him ' not to
" despair of living,' and said, ' he trusted that Divine
" Providence would restore him once more to his dear
" country and friends.' ' Ah, Doctor !' he replied, ' it is
" all over, it is all over !'

" Many messages were sent to Captain Hardy by the
" surgeon, requesting his attendance on his lordship,
" who had become impatient, and often exclaimed :—
" ' Will no one bring Hardy to me? He must be
" killed, he is surely destroyed !' The captain's aide-
" de-camp now came below (Mr. Bulkeley), and stated,
" ' that circumstances respecting the fleet required
" Hardy's presence on deck, but that he would avail
" himself of the first favourable moment to come.'

" On hearing him say this to the surgeon, Nelson
" asked, ' Who had brought it ?' ' It is Mr. Bulkeley,
" . . .' said Mr. Burke. ' It is his voice,' said
" Nelson ; and then to Bulkeley, ' remember me to your
" father.'

"After about an hour and ten minutes Hardy came.
"They shook hands affectionately, and then Nelson
"said, 'Well, Hardy, how goes the battle? How goes
"the day with us?' 'Very well, my lord; we have got
"twelve or fourteen of the enemy's ships in our
"possession; but five of their van have tacked, and
"show an intention of bearing down on the 'Victory.'
"I have, therefore, called two or three fresh ships
"round us, and have no doubt of giving them a good
"drubbing.' 'I hope,' said Nelson, 'none of *our* ships
"have struck, Hardy!' 'No, my lord, there is no fear
"of that.' Nelson then said, 'Hardy, I am a dead man,
"Hardy; I am going fast; it will be all over with me
"soon. Come near to me.' . . . . Mr. Burke was
"about to withdraw at the beginning of this conversa-
"tion, but Nelson perceiving his intention, desired him
"to remain. Captain Hardy observed 'that he hoped
"Mr. Beatty could hold out some prospect of life.'
"'Oh, no, it is impossible. My back is shot through.
"Beatty will tell you so.' After a parting shake of the
"hand, Hardy returned to the deck.
" "About fifty minutes after, Hardy returned. They
"again shook hands, and while the Captain retained
"Nelson's hand, he congratulated him, even in the arms
"of death, on his brilliant victory, which, he said, was
"complete; though he did not know how many of the
"enemy were captured, as it was impossible to perceive
"each ship distinctly. He was certain, however, of
"fourteen or fifteen having surrendered. 'That is
"well, but I bargained for twenty;' and then, emphati-
"cally, *Anchor*, Hardy, *Anchor*.' To this Hardy
"replied: "I suppose, my lord, Admiral Collingwood
"will now take upon himself the direction of affairs?'
"'Not while I live, I hope, Hardy,' cried the dying
"chief, and at that moment tried ineffectually to raise
"himself from his bed. 'No,' added he, 'do *you*
"anchor, Hardy.' 'Shall we make the signal, sir?'

" ' Yes, for if I live, I'll anchor.'   He then told Captain
" Hardy ' he felt in a few minutes he should be no
" more,' adding in low tone, ' Don't throw me over-
" board.'   ' Oh, no, certainly not,' replied Hardy.
" ' Then you know what to do, . . . kiss me,
" Hardy.'   The Captain now knelt down and kissed
" his cheek, when Nelson said : ' Now I am satisfied ;
" thank God I have done my duty.'   Hardy stood for
" a moment or two in silent contemplation ; he knelt
" down again, and kissed his lordship's forehead.
" Nelson said, ' Who is that ?'   ' It is Hardy,' answered
" the Captain. . ' God bless you, Hardy.'   After this
" . . . . Hardy withdrew, and returned to the
" quarter-deck."

His chaplain, Dr. Scott, records thus his last moments : —

" After this, the Admiral was perfectly tranquil,
" looking at me in his accustomed manner when
" alluding to any prior discourse.   ' I have not been
" a great sinner, doctor,' said he. . . . . The
" confusion of the scene, the pain endured by the hero,
" and the necessity of alleviating his sufferings by
" giving lemonade to quench his thirst, and by rubbing
" his body, of course precluded the reading of prayers
" to him in a regular form, but otherwise during the
" three hours-and-a-half of Nelson's mortal agony they
" ejaculated short prayers together, and Nelson
" frequently said ' pray for me, Doctor.'   Every interval,
" indeed, allowed by the intense pain, and not taken
" up in the conduct of the action, or in the mention of
" his own private affairs, was thus employed in low and
" earnest supplications for Divine mercy.   The last
" words which Dr. Scott heard murmured on his lips
" were ' God, and my country,' and he passed so quietly
" out of life that Scott, who had been occupied ever
" since he had been brought below, in all the offices of
" the most tender nurse, was still rubbing (him) when
" the surgeon perceived that all was over."

Thus he died, uttering with his last breath the words which had been from first to last the Lode Star of his life. Truly religious, his veneration unsullied by cant, brave to a fault, loyal and faithful to his King, country, and friends; frank and open in every relation of his life:—assuredly there is no character and career in history which can be studied and understood with greater benefit than those of Nelson.

The summary given by Captain Brenton in the third volume of his work, and quoted in " James's Naval History," is too admirable to be passed over, and should be inserted here; he says:—

" Thus fell the greatest sea officer of this or any " other nation recorded in history; his talents, his " courage, his fidelity, his zeal, his love for his King and " country, were exceeded by none. Never had any " man the happy intuitive faculty of seizing the moment " of propitious fortune equal to Nelson. His whole " career, from his earliest entrance into the service, " offers to the youth of the British Navy the most " illustrious examples of every manly virtue; whether " we view him as a midshipman, a lieutenant, as the " captain of a frigate, or a commander-in-chief. We " have seen him as captain of the ' Agamemnon ' in " Larma Bay, writing his despatches while his ship lay " aground in an enemy's port; we have seen him as " captain of a 74 gun ship, on the 14th of February, " lay a Spanish first-rate and an 84 gun ship on board, " and with his little band of heroes rush from ship to " ship and take them both. Equally great in the hour of " defeat as of victory, see him at Teneriffe with his " shattered arm going to the rescue of his companions " and saving their lives, while every moment of delay " increased the peril of his own by hemorrhage and " exhaustion; see him walk up the ship's side, hear him

" command the surgeon to proceed to amputation, and
" see the fortitude with which he bore the agonizing
" pain. Follow him to the Nile, and contemplate the
" destruction of the fleet of France and the consequent
" loss of her vast army led by Buonaparte. How great
" was his professional knowledge at Copenhagen, when,
" despising death, he refused to obey the signal of
" recall, because he knew that by such obedience his
" country would have been disgraced, the great object
" of the expedition frustrated, and Britain, overpowered
" by the increased energy of the northern confederacy,
" might have sunk under the multiplied force of her
" enemies.

" See him on the same occasion sit down in the
" midst of carnage and address a letter to the Crown
" Prince of Denmark, which, while it gave a victory to
" his country, added to her glory by stopping the
" useless effusion of human blood. We have seen him
" the patient, watchful, and anxious guardian of our
" honor in the Mediterranean, where, for two years, he
" sought an opportunity to engage an enemy of
" superior force.

" Three times we have seen him pursue the foe of his
" country to Egypt, and once to the West Indies. And
" these great steps he took entirely on his own responsi-
" bility, disregarding any personal consideration, any
" calculation of force, or any allurement of gain.

" Coming, at last, to the termination of his glorious
" career, the end of his life was worthy of all his other
" deeds ; the battle of Trafalgar will stand, without the
" aid of sculpture or painting, the greatest memorial of
" British valour ever exhibited ; no pen can do justice,
" no description can convey, an adequate idea of the
" glories of that day ; and the event, which deprived us
" of our favourite chief, consummated his earthly fame,
" and rendered his name for ever dear to his country.
" Had not his transcendent virtues been shaded by a

" fault, we might have been accused of flattery. No
" human being was ever perfect, and however we may
" regret the blemish in the affair Caracciolo, we must
" ever acknowledge that the character of Nelson, as a
" public servant, is not exceeded in the history of the
" world."

Happily this last paragraph can now be refuted, for
Professor Laughton, in the introduction to his " Letters and
Despatches of Lord Nelson," recently published, says, that
of the—

" Many persistent misrepresentations which have
" clung to Nelson's history, . . . there is one which
" strikes at his character as a man of probity and
" honour, and demands a closer investigation—it is that
" which relates to his doings in the Bay of Naples, in
" June, 1799."

After giving his reasons and the evidence on which they
are based, Professor Laughton utterly disposes of these
" misrepresentations," and among them that especially
relating to the execution of Caracciolo.

As, on this point, other late biographers are in accord
with Professor Laughton, this " blemish " must now
disappear.

It is, indeed, a deplorable fact that such misconceptions
should have ever been allowed to exist, but now that
reliable evidence has been disinterred, and we are able to
read and to judge for ourselves, we discover how totally
opposed such " misrepresentations " are to the feelings and
principles which, by his own writings and actions, we find
solely to have governed Nelson's whole life.

If this incongruity strike the reader, and so make some of
the slanders and misconceptions formerly disseminated
about him impossible of belief, this little book will not have
been compiled in vain.

APPENDIX.

A short account of the Estate or Duchy of Bronte since it was so created may appropriately be added here, for interest must always be attached to it, as the gift to Lord Nelson by the King of Naples.

Its present increasing prosperity forms also a most interesting contrast to the condition in which it was when Lord Nelson received it. As has been partially seen, it gave him considerable trouble, and he derived but little, if any, substantial benefit from it. By his Will it passed to his brother William (the first Earl Nelson), and again through his daughter it has descended with the title to the late Viscount Bridport, Duke of Bronte, and now to his son, the Honourable Alexander Nelson Hood, under whose care and that of his father, Bronte has attained a prosperity and an influence which Lord Nelson is known to have desired for it. but which, under the expense and trouble it cost him, he must have ceased to expect.

In the paper which Mr. Hood contributed to the " Nelson " of Mr. G. Lathom Browne, we have a short history of the Estate, from which, and also from a series of reports sent to the Home Government by Mr. Stigand (British Consul at Palermo) on different subjects relating to the Island of Sicily, the following extracts and summary are taken.

The Duchy of Bronte is situated in the province of Catania, about thirty miles from the eastern, about the same distance from the northern, coast of Sicily. Mr. Hood writes : —

" It is of great extent, but not so large as when granted to
" Lord Nelson by Ferdinand IV. of Naples. It was then
" encumbered by vexatious claims on the part of the
" township of Bronte, to settle which a portion of the
" property had ultimately to be ceded as the price of peace.
" It contains vineyards, and arable lands which grow
" magnificent crops of wheat, and lava lands which produce
" the valuable pistachio nut, the olive, and the almond.
" Orange groves flourish in the more sheltered parts.
" Forests of oak and beech stretch away many miles on

" the sides of the mountains, which rise six thousand feet
" above the sea level, and from that altitude a magnificent
" panorama of Etna and its countless parasitic cones is
" obtained on the one hand, while on the other lies the blue
" Mediterranean, dotted with the isles of Lipari, sparkling
" like jewels on its surface.

" The country is very beautiful and a marvel of fertility.
" The climate is genial, though winter brings frost and
" snow."

The Castello di Maniace is the principal seat of the family,
and the administration of the Duchy.

The name of Maniace was given to the surrounding country
in commemoration of a victory gained over the Saracens by the
Byzantine general, George Maniaces, about A.D. 1032.

He built the Castle, about which a small town sprung up.

Later the Castle was converted into a monastery in 1173 by
Queen Margaret of Sicily, and was inhabited by monks of divers
orders, in order to guard a miraculous picture of the Madonna
still present in the church.

By the rights and privileges of this Royal foundation—and
these still belong to the Dukes of Bronte—Lord Nelson enjoyed
that of full ecclesiastical jurisdiction over the church and
territory.

" The church remains much the same as when it was
" built. The pointed Norman arches of the interior, and
" windows of the same period, are architecturally interesting,
" as is also, and artistically, the beautiful door, with its
" marble and granite pillars, ornate capitals, and deep
" mouldings. Immense granaries, wine cellars, and store
" houses, with the monks' kitchen and cells, now turned to
" modern uses, surround two spacious court-yards. . . .
" . . . The muniment rooms contain many ancient docu-
" ments, dating from A.D. 900, which are full of monkish lore
" and legal cunning.

" Among them is the hero's will."

The Castello stands alone on the slope of Etna, about four
miles from the nearest village, and some eight miles from the
town of Bronte, and is built on a mass of lava rock which so
divides the confluents of the river Simeto that the streams flow
on two sides of it.

This river may at times be more appropriately called an impetuous torrent, and was the ancient river Symœthus.

"When the estate was erected into a Duchy and handed
"over to Nelson,' says Mr. Stigand, 'it was in a bare and
"wretched plight. It was forty miles distant from any
"carriage road, and no proprietor had lived on it for more
"than two hundred years. After the flight of the last
"monastic proprietors, from 1693 to 1799, the property was
"in the hands of caretakers. Reforms and improvements
"were commenced on the estate soon after Nelson received
"it, but little was done on a grand scale until the succession
"of the present Duke in 1868. . . . . Roads were
"immediately commenced; Mr. Hood had the satisfaction
"of being the first to drive down to Maniace in 1873, and
"there are now fifteen miles of roads on the property. Farm-
"houses have been repaired and built, several bridges over
"torrents (at times impassable) have been erected, and the
"Castello itself restored and enlarged, not only to make a
"suitable dwelling-house according to English notions, but
"also to allow for storage of grain and wine, and for
"stabling. One of the chief events in the history of the
"improvements which are going on, was the introduction of
"a ten horse-power traction engine from England. Its
"journey up to Maniace through Linguaglossa, Randezzo,
"and other places, under the conduct of Mr. Nelson Hood
"as chief engine-driver, excited a commotion in the country,
"the memory of which survives as something quite out of
"the common."

It would seem that although some moral advancement has taken place among the people, it has hardly kept pace with the material improvements enumerated above. Notwithstanding that, there is much in the following details, as recited by Mr. Hood, which must give pleasure to read. He writes:—

"Life in this Duchy of Bronte is comparatively easy.
"Though a kind of feudal state is maintained, and *campieri*,
"or mounted guards, in uniforms of red and blue with silver
"facings, the Bronte colors, protect the family when in
"Sicily, and the property on all occasions, there is much
"kindliness of feeling between employer and employed.
"Dependents pass a lifetime in the service of the Duchy,

" and there died but recently one who had worked for nearly
" eighty years as dairyman on the property.

"The jealousy of a foreigner, that might be expected on
" the part of the nation, does not exist here. Trust and
" confidence in English integrity are manifested by tenants
" and servants alike; and it is not unfrequently that the
" former leave their receipts for rent unasked for, as willingly
" as they accept the consignment of payments in kind
" without questioning the measure or the measurer. The
" people do not repose the same confidence in their fellow
" countrymen. It is difficult to give a correct idea of the
" character of the lower and middle classes of Sicilians,
" perhaps without dwelling somewhat harshly on their short-
" comings, ... where redemption from slavery is
" but recent, a true conception of liberty may not be
" expected.

"Liberated but yesterday from the thraldom of a super-
" stition as gross as can well be imagined, and from an
" ignorant priesthood, the people have yet to learn the value
" of veracity and straightforwardness. . . . . But the
" people are hardworking and diligent, and when their own
" interests are not too deeply involved they are kindly
" disposed and affectionate. . . . . . Since 1868
" much has been done to improve the property. . . . .
" Steam machinery and saw mills have been introduced into
" the forests.

"The superannuated dependents pass a peaceful old age
" with suitable pensions; and the spiritual requirements of
" the neighbourhood are provided for by the weekly celebra-
" tion of Mass in the old church, built, as has before been
" said, by Queen Margaret."

The principal existing source of revenue, and one which now
promises rapidly to increase still more, is that of the " Duchy of
Bronte " wine, of which Mr. Stigand gives a most interesting
account, but one which from its length cannot, in its entirety, be
inserted here.

He speaks of the cellars where—

"The tuns or casks are stored in imposing array; the
" largest tun has the majestic name of 'La Madre,' and
" bears it on her face in the largest of capitals; it contains
" 3,344 gallons, or 18,200 bottles, and a good sized dinner

" party might be accommodated in its interior when empty,
" if a floor were put to it. There are, besides, two
" enormous vats, closed at the top, which are, in fact, also
" casks, but of a different shape, and these are about double
" the size of ' La Madre,' and capable of containing together
" 60,000 bottles, besides which there are 20 casks of 1,600
" gallons, and 120 of smaller dimensions."

Mr. Stigand then describes the process of the wine-making;
how the grapes are sifted from the stalks, and prepared by the
feet, but how, at Bronte, the most careful precautions are taken
that the feet should be shod in large gutta percha mocassins,
which are thoroughly washed morning and evening.

From the pressing house the juice runs in continuous streams
through caoutchouc tubes into reservoirs placed in the adjacent
compartment, where the first fermentation is allowed to proceed.

After the first fermentation the juice is transferred to the
larger vats, is—

" Allowed to clear, and subjected carefully to the ordinary
" process of racking and refining three or four times a year
" for about seven years. The casks for final lodgment of
" the wine are prepared with all possible care, and each one
" is subjected to severe scrutiny before the wine is sent forth
" for exportation.
" These casks are prepared on the *stabilimento* itself, and
" from wood coming from the estate."

The vineyard is calculated to produce, under ordinary fair
conditions, 180,000 bottles a year.

" The wine is of a light amber colour, dry, of pleasant
" bouquet, of a good aroma, with full natural body, and is
" esteemed beneficial for invalids ; it is lighter than Marsala,
" with something of a flavour between Madeira and
" Sauterne. It is said to keep any time, and to improve in
" bottle."

Such then is the existing condition of the estate of Bronte,
and when we regard the progress which has been made under the
expenditure and care of its past and present owners and sons,
we may remember the wish of Lord Nelson that, " all on the
estate should enjoy happiness and prosperity," and believe, as
far as human possibilities permit, that wish to be now fulfilled.

It remains only to add that on Christmas Eve, 1890, was erected in the courtyard of the Castle of Maniace, a cross in memory of Lord Nelson. The grey lava stone taken from the quarries, and begun and finished by the workmen on the estate, has been hewn into a large monolith cross, from the design and under the superintendence of the Honourable Alexander Nelson Hood. It stands sixteen feet high, and on the monolith pedestal are inscribed the words, "Heroi Immortali Nili." It was unveiled by Mr. Hood, who, speaking in Italian, after touching upon the principal deeds of his Great Uncle, concluded:—

"Notwithstanding friends left at home, and the immediate "triumph among his companions-in-arms, following on his "remarkable victory—notwithstanding the welcome and the "fresh honours that would have awaited him in England, "his last thoughts on his death-bed reverted to the standing "rule of his life, devotion to his King and country, which "found expression in the last words that he uttered. "'Thank God! I have done my duty.'"

CPSIA information can be obtained
at www.ICGtesting.com
Printed in the USA
BVOW06s1013250917
495833BV00021B/343/P

9 781333 169152